Women, the Elderly and Social Policy in Finland and Japan

The Muse or the Worker Bee?

Edited by
BRIITTA KOSKIAHO

in cooperation with
Paula Mäkinen and Maija-Liisa Pättiniemi

Avebury

Aldershot • Brookfield USA • Hong Kong • Singapore • Sydney

Published by
Avebury
Ashgate Publishing Limited
Gower House
Croft Road
Aldershot
Hants GU11 3HR
England

Ashgate Publishing Company
Old Post Road
Brookfield
Vermont 05036
USA

British Library Cataloguing in Publication Data

Women, the Elderly and Social Policy
in Finland and Japan: The Muse or the
Worker Bee?
    I. Koskiaho, Briitta
    305.42094897

    ISBN 1 85628 859 5

Library of Congress Catalog Card Number: 95-80357

Printed and bound by Athenaeum Press, Ltd.,
Gateshead, Tyne & Wear.

Contents

List of tables and figures

Preface

The economic rise of Japan and other Asian countries has rekindled the interest of European scholars in the societies and cultures of Eastern and Southeastern Asia. Our future is not only tied to the European Union and the USA, but also and especially to the new economic and political conglomerate of the states of Eastern and Southeastern Asia. The last to wake up were the social scientists. Traditionally we have been interested in the societies of economic powers, but not until such power has become more than obvious. So far few Finnish social scientists have taken any interest in the study of the Japanese, Chinese or Korean societies before the 1990s. This may of course be due to the language barrier. In order to obtain a true picture of a foreign society the researcher needs to communicate with the local population and make use of locally produced documentary material. You will not get very far by relying solely on secondary sources.

A useful research strategy could be to import scientists from one country to the other, or to conduct simultaneous research in both countries with comparative results presented jointly. These are the strategies that the Department of Social Policy and Social Work at the University of Tampere in Finland has been employing. By providing one of the main subjects in the Japanese Studies Programme (Faculty of Social Sciences, International School of Social Sciences) we also hope to educate new researchers of our own. One of the collaborators in this task has been the University of Vienna and its Japanese studies scholars. The comparative approach has made it possible for us to compile this publication.

In the prolonged gestation period of this book, a considerable number of people have provided the stimulation for it in Austria, Finland, Great Britain and Japan. The Editors are grateful to all these people, too numerous to be mentioned separately, for their kind support and comments. Two women deserve to be mentioned by name, however. We extend our warmest thanks to Liisa Ritanen for checking the language and style of the text, and to Aila Helin for the word processing.

Introduction: Finland and Japan, two late-developers

Briitta Koskiaho

Old manufacturing industries in Finland, such as textile and metal industries, experienced a structural change in the mid-1970s. The work force diminished drastically, and old machines and factories were abandoned. Factories were closed down, or their production was transferred abroad or to new locations in Finland. After such changes the production frequently ground to a halt. The life in former industrial localities with a one-sided industrial base was of course severely affected by this process. The general economic recession, which started at the beginning of the 1990s, accelerated this process and extended the consequences of the structural changes to the service sector.

The industrial developments in Japan have largely taken place simultaneously with the corresponding developments in Finland. In both countries, large-scale industries started with cotton industry; in Finland around 1830 and in Japan during the Meiji period when Japan had opened up to the outside world. The prime concern of the ruling classes from the 1860s onwards was to get the economy in tune with the new times. Technical experts from England were invited to Japan, and Japanese apprentices were sent to England. As a result, production methods of large-scale industries were brought to Japan. The child and female work force of the textile industry became the most prominent forerunners of industrialization at the end of the 19th century. In Finland a similar development took place. The industrialization of Japan at the end of the 19th century thus rested on the shoulders of the female work force in the cotton and silk factories.

1

Gradually the heavy industry overtook the light industry as far as the value of the production was concerned. Despite this, women made up the majority of the total work force in Japan even at the beginning of the next century. The majority of these female workers were again so-called cotton and silk girls. The traditionally male-dominated industrial sectors, such as steel, coal, mining and shipbuilding industries, began to develop rapidly at the turn of the century. In Finland the male-dominated industry, in particular the paper and pulp industry and the iron and metal industry, developed a little earlier.

In both countries the structures of the old heavy and light industries began to erode at the same time. A steady renewal had taken place during the first half of the 20th century, but the peak of this development occurred in the 1970s. Korea and Taiwan started competing with Japan. Other rising industrial nations in East Asia and Southeast Asia with cheap labour costs joined in this competition. The same competition extended further and shook the foundations of the old industries in Europe. In Finland, as well as in Japan, the high domestic costs of production became more of a problem in view of the increasingly severe competition. The factors which were considered the most important in this respect were the salary costs and the various benefits of the workers.

Japan has already become the prime mover in the East Asian and Southeast Asian economic zone. In addition, Japan competes with the United States. The country is also taking on the role of a financier in the developing countries, equal in importance to that of the United States. Japanese investors have already conquered all parts of the world from north to south and from east to west. The factor underlying this success has been the fairly uniform social structure of the country, as well as the multi-layered and diversified structure of its economy. Finland belongs to the Nordic zone of welfare states, where economic development was strong during the whole of the 1980s. With the beginning of the 1990s, a very deep economic recession took place in Finland. This was largely a consequence of the weak international economic situation during the same period, which was also felt in Japan at the beginning of the 1990s.

In the postwar period both Finland and Japan have experienced different developments as far as the labour is concerned. In Finland the volume of female labour has risen to a level nearly equal to that of the male labour, whereas in Japan the women are now of less importance in the large-scale industries as a consequence of the decreased need for workers in the textile industry from the 1930s onwards. In big companies the regular work force consists almost exclusively of male workers. Women are employed on a temporary basis, as part-time workers or for a few years prior to marriage or the birth of their first child. The cotton girls of yesteryears correspond to present-day part-time workers or so-called office ladies who are busy running back and forth between their home and their office. These workers are young ladies who are employed for a few years after their two-year academic female studies and are taken on to perform various secretarial and office duties.

The framework for the economic developments in Japan after the Second World War included a role for women which can be characterized as a model embracing the functions of housewife and mother. The housewife model has its roots in the ideals of the 1930s, at the time typical in Europe, too. Despite the fact that women had to do men's work during the war, they were sent off to their homes after the war. The housewife ideal has not been realized in practice, however. Its realization has been the most successful in upper middle class families. Fifty per cent, or even more, of the women at working age participate in working life. However, this participation mostly takes place through temporary or part-time employment which is not regulated by the rules and agreements usually required for regular work. The public measures which would make it easier for women to participate in working life are largely absent, since 'officially' women are expected to spend their time at home. This means that the women play a secondary role in working life; women participate in *secondary labour markets*. This participation takes on many forms, some of which are indicative of exploitation and canalization of work, while others enhance the independence and mobility of women (Mary Sato, Women in the Japanese Workplace. London 1990; Dorinne K. Kondo, Crafting Selves. Power, Gender, and Discourses of Identity in a Japanese Workplace. Chicago 1990).

During the rapid economic development in the 1980s the demand for trained women grew as a result of the shortage of qualified labour. Young women began to make plans for their career, which resembled the lifelong career developments of western women. The economic recession of the 1990s made an abrupt end of this

3

development and put the women back to their more or less traditional position in society.

An oriental smile, a polite subservience and withdrawal from public life. This is the superficial conception of the Japanese woman, who is principally concerned with life within the boundaries of her home. Such stereotypic conceptions are always dangerous, especially when they concern inhabitants in countries which are in some sense peripheral, as viewed from more central regions in the world. Both Finland and Japan are considered to belong to such peripheral regions. Individual variations among women in Japan are indeed large, perhaps even larger than among the men with a career-oriented life.

Despite the fact that in Finland, too, the important role of women at home was emphasized, the women remained in the labour market after the war. This gradually led to a totally different view of the position of women in society compared with Japan. In Finland men and women participate in working life in equal numbers and more than 80 per cent of the women with at least one child under 18 years of age are wage earners. Yet even in Finland the labour market has been criticized for being different for women and men. As care has been transferred outside the home and has become a social benefit, people engaged in this type of work are mainly women. In different circumstances the same women would probably take care of children and the elderly at home. Women have, however, conquered new sectors of working life. They study at universities and take the same degrees as men. In many fields of study women already outnumber men and the majority of university graduates today are women.

In her study on the process of becoming a professional woman Maaret Wagner refers to academic women who transform their identity in order to combine their old feminine identity with the new professional identity in the Finnish society (Maaret Wagner, Constructions of Femininity in Academic Women. Annales Academiæ Scientiarum Fennicæ, Ser. B, Tom. 275. Helsinki 1994). Female university graduates, especially young women under the age of forty, do not wish to identify themselves with academic dons, who are mainly interested in academic merits and power. In terms of their career, these women find the concept of success quite problematic, especially if they try to combine their career and their family and caring obligations. Wagner, however, refers to the

4

conceptions of feminism which are constantly under change in the changing society.

In Finland the participation of women in working life has been facilitated by the provision of adequate social services, organized and financed by public authorities. At the same time efforts have been made to change working life in the direction of allowing not only mothers but also fathers to stay at home for specific periods in order to take care of small children. Since the beginning of the 1980s this practice has slowly gained acceptance among young families. When the degree of participation of women in working life is high, one also needs services provided by society in order to take care of the problems related to elderly people. The question of caring for the elderly has indeed been accepted as a societal responsibility in the Nordic countries. Although the immediate family normally participates in caring for their elderly people, this participation is usually restricted to light work only. The main responsibility has more and more been transferred to the public service sector for the elderly. In the Nordic countries, the children's legal obligations to take care of their old parents was removed a long time ago, contrary to the situation in Japan.

The global economic recession in the 1990s has changed the above picture in Finland. Financial difficulties on both the state and the municipal level have in just a few years since the beginning of the 1990s led to a restrictive attitude towards public spending. Social benefits and especially social services have become a target of criticism. This makes it more difficult for women to participate in working life as full-time wage earners. The restructuring of industry during the previous decade had already diminished the number of male workers in heavy industry (John Doling et al. (eds.), Restructuring in Old Industrial Towns in Finland. University of Tampere, Department of Social Policy and Social Work. Research Report, Series A, No. 6. Tampere 1994).

At the beginning of the 1990s, unemployment became an issue of growing concern for women. The abolition of services meant that the number of full-time female jobs in society decreased. In the private sector, primarily in retail trade, more and more workers were employed on a part-time basis, which has had an adverse effect on the number of full-time female jobs. Among the Nordic countries, Finland has had the smallest number of part-time employees. At the end of the 1980s ten per cent of the workers were

5

employed in part-time jobs, but now the number of part-time employees is increasing steadily. Hence one can argue that the positions of the Japanese and the Finnish women in the labour market have started to converge.

The economy has a direct bearing on the role of women in the labour market and on how old workers are phased out from active work. More generally, it is also reflected in how society treats elderly people. The livelihood of elderly people and their need for services, or more specifically, how elderly people live and who takes care of those in need of help, are once more issues directly related to the role of women in society. During the period of expansion, which started after the Second World War and which seems to have ended by the beginning of the 1990s, these questions were settled differently in Japan and in Finland.

The life expectancy of the Japanese is the longest in the world together with the inhabitants of Iceland. The percentage of elderly people grows faster in Japan on the average than in any other country in the world. Finland comes close to Japan in this respect. In both countries the percentage in question is still lower than in many countries in Central Europe. The statistical 'care potential' of women (the total number of individuals needing care in relation to the number of women) is of crucial importance in Japan as far as the care of both children and elderly people is concerned. Voluntary work has long traditions, in the cities too, dating back to the old village communities. Volunteers also help elderly people who live alone, taking care of their practical problems. Many of the volunteers participating in this work are old men, not just women. Nevertheless, the status of women and their relation to work is decisive as far as the increasing need for care is concerned, which in turn is caused by the expected increase in the proportion of elderly people in society. The average number of children is decreasing all the time, so dramatical changes in the care potential are not expected. The situation of care potential outlined above provides a valid picture of the situation in Finland, too.

The collapse of the economy of advanced countries has led to growing insecurity in the world, especially in regions of military instability. Meanwhile neo-liberal ideology has gained increasing support in many countries including the Nordic countries which for decades have maintained political coalitions advocating *the collective welfare state ideology*. The private sector is becoming more important as far as social policies are concerned, which goes against the traditional welfare state ideology. This has also changed the vocabulary of social policy researchers in the Nordic countries. *Privatisation of services and entrepreneurship* have become the order of the day, replacing the idea of state-supported institutions and services. These concepts, which until recently were totally unknown in this context, pose new theoretical and empirical challenges for researchers of social policy in Finland.

In Japan a declared welfare state ideology has been an almost unknown concept both in the research and practice of social policy. The Japanese society has always been characterized by a mixture of confidence in the new form of society and anxiety over the loss of traditional cultural qualities and values. Are these two approaches to social policy now coming closer to each other? To evaluate this question, the authors of the articles in this publication have depicted the Finnish and Japanese societies and their social policies from a specific point of view, namely focusing on women and elderly people. All of the authors are female researchers. Yet this work does not represent any particular school of thought in women's studies, but rather considers women and elderly people from the point of view of change in society and implementation of social policy.

The researchers of the Finnish society are all Finnish citizens living in Finland. On the one hand, they concentrate on the life of women and families in *Finland* and, on the other hand, on the position and conditions of elderly people, especially old women. *Mirja Tolkki-Nikkonen* analyses the Finnish family system. Her article is based on two studies of the same families, with an interval of fifteen years between them. She discusses family structure, social relations, essential characteristics of the family and position of females in different family types. *Liisa Knuuti* examines postmodern consciousness and young female urban life styles, especially in the capital city of Finland, where a new urban middle class life style in well-paid occupational groups is visible. *Maija-Liisa Pättiniemi* analyses social services for elderly people in urban conditions. The author summarises the results of empirical studies on elderly women in Tampere and describes public and semi-public house-based services which seem to divide elderly people into two different classes. She also discusses voluntary work in social welfare institutions. As a particular case, she considers old retired

7

female textile workers who rely on institutional care for the elderly.

The authors of the articles on *Japan* are partly Japanese female researchers and partly European ones, among them a Finnish specialist Raija Hashimoto who has lived in Japan for two decades. In her article *Briitta Koskiaho* analyses the housewife institution, the housing and home centred life and the working life of women. She also discusses the problems related to comparisons between Eastern and Western cultural spheres. *Machiko Osawa* concentrates on the problems related to female occupations and economic compensations of social security and taxation as well as the possibilities of getting family services in the Japanese society. *Sachiko Matsumura* examines the living conditions of elderly people and their sources of livelihood. Special attention has been given to gender differences. Relations between coping and social services are in the focus of the article of *Ingrid Getreuer-Kargl*. The ageing society has been recognized as a major problem of the Japanese society; it has dominated social political planning in the last few years. In the European context, in planning services for the elderly, the fact that there is a larger number of females than males is taken into account. In contrast, attention in the Japanese society concentrates on the problems of old males. The article highlights the consequences of this attitude in planning. Finally, in her articles *Raija Hashimoto* illustrates some crucial characteristics of institutional care and voluntary work among elderly people in Japan, especially in the Greater Tokyo area.

People reproduce the social structures of their societies. In a global community this does not only take place within one society, but the whole global community participates in the process. Those societies which are economically and politically more powerful than others have traditionally been in a position to transform the other societies according to their own interests, as shown by the period of colonialism, for example. As we approach the turn of the century, new centres of power emerge in the global community. One of these power centres appears in Eastern and Southeastern Asia. The old European communities have joined together more tightly than before forming economic and political bonds. The future will show, whether the Asian economic and political cooperation will give rise to a new female type and whether this differs from its European counterpart.

Inside Europe there is a clear tendency to strive for unification of the position of women in society. The self-sufficient and independent woman of Northern Europe will have to compete with the woman of Central Europe who has traditionally been oriented towards home and family centred activities. On the other hand, female activists in Europe have respected the women of Northern Europe and their position in their respective societies. The future developments will to a large extent be dependent on how the women themselves can influence their own position and participate in the shaping of the new integrated European community.

Part One
FINLAND

1 The woman and the family in Finland

Mirja Tolkki-Nikkonen

The rules of normality in family life are established by ideas and practices, or if you like, by paradigms that prevail at any given time. However, these paradigms are also vulnerable to change when existing rules begin to fail, when anomalies can no longer be evaded, when 'normality' is challenged by the real world of everyday experience. At any historical moment there are competing families — some hegemonic, others marginalized or stigmatized. Most of our talk about families is, however, clouded by unexplored notions of what families really are like. We confuse the ideal with the real.

In recent years the concept of the family has been at the centre of heated debate both in academic research and in social policy contexts. The idea of 'the family' or 'the nuclear family' has remarkable strength and power — it is something that just about any member of our society can define. It has also been enforced by state politics. The image of the family has been quite clear: a married heterosexual couple with children.

Although the tendency in the scientific debate has been to deconstruct abstract conceptions such as the family (e.g. Lorber & Farrell 1991) and to accept the diversity and variety of families, the norm in social and fiscal policy has always been the 'normal' family.

In Finland, the recent changes in the family structure were preceded by rapid changes in the social structure. During 1960-1975 the industrial structure changed radically, while the rural-urban migration was at its height at around the same time. Between 1967

13

and 1975 the family structure also changed significantly, with a substantial increase in divorces, consensual unions, remarriages, and a decrease in the average number of children.

Given the changes that have taken place in the family structure in Finland, it would clearly be wrong to speak about 'the family', which as a concept has rather strong ideological undertones. To resolve this conceptual ambiguity and its practical consequences in fiscal and social policy, different committees in Finland have now been attempting to redefine the family. What is the proper unit of definition? Could the family be defined as a group of people sharing the same refrigerator? Single parent families and individuals obliged to pay child support now have their own organizations to defend their interests; the latter would also like to be defined as a family with children. It has also been suggested that motherhood should be redefined, and recently even a society for 'new family culture' was established.

What is the family?

The traditional, monolithic concept of the family is typically employed at a high level of abstraction; rather than revealing historically and culturally distinct arrangements, the term actually hides these from view. Redefinitions have been suggested along three different lines:

a) We need a broader definition than the traditional family model of the married heterosexual couple with children. The definition should also incorporate consensual unions, single-parent families, remarriages, etc. The family could be any unit in which at least one adult and one child are living together.

This kind of expansion is often embedded in and tied to the traditional family model, much in the same way as the popular conception of sexuality is tied to marital sexuality through such terms as premarital, extramarital and postmarital sexuality.

b) We should altogether discard the concept of the family because it is biased (Bernandes 1988). We should instead explore the meanings attached to the family by everyday actors and the way in which the actors generate and sustain these meanings. This, however, is only possible if we deliberately avoid referring to the family ourselves.

14

c) We should define the family in different ways in different contexts (Liss 1987; Trost 1988). 'Rather than settling for a particular definition, it seems more appropriate to define families according to the particular issues involved. For example, policies concerned with the socialization of children should use a definition households with children. In sum, definitions of the family should be relative to the issue at hand rather than sacrosanct.' (Liss 1987, 796)

This is in fact what happens in everyday life; we define the family in different ways in different contexts. There is no 'real', objectively defined family, only different ways of talking about the family. And it is precisely through these discourses that we create the family. We are no longer concerned with finding out who the members of the family are, who live in the same household, or what the functions of the family are; our attention shifts to practical, interpretative issues which are tied to the varied conditions of understanding the family. Gubrium (1987) has observed that the nature of the family varies greatly according to the context in which it is studied. This means that the family consists of the way in which we talk about it in different contexts.

First image of the Finnish families: Structure

According to the statistical criteria so far employed in Finland (criteria are under change), the family consists of persons living in the same household and representing no more than two generations; if there are three or more generations in the same household, the family consists of the two youngest. So who, on the basis of this definition, do not count as a family?

Extended families consisting of two or more nuclear families are rare in Finland: in 1980 they accounted for about one per cent of all households in urban municipalities and for three per cent in rural municipalities. Extended families including some relative — usually a grandmother — are somewhat more common. However, extended families, together with certain other forms of restructured families, are excluded from family statistics; they are not counted as families but as households. The same applies to single people living alone. About 60 per cent of all Finnish people who do not belong to a family live alone. The number of single persons has increased from 18.5 per cent in 1950 to 28.2 per cent in 1985. Two thirds of

15

them are women, of whom nearly 60 per cent are divorced or widowed.

It has been estimated that at the end of 1987, restructured families accounted for 8 per cent of families with children and for 3 per cent of all families. In 1990, 7 per cent of families with children were restructured families. In every other restructured family, all children living at home were descendants of only one or the other party to the couple relationship. (Saari & Sauli 1990)

Today, about 15 per cent of all Finnish families are single-parent families, and 87 per cent of these are mother-only families. About half of the latter are the result of a divorce but more and more often they are deliberate choices by the women themselves — women who are financially independent. It is now more acceptable for women to have children alone, without the children being called illegitimate bastards.

There has been some tendency to overestimate the population of the new family forms. For example, it is often argued that a unit consisting of my, your and our children is *the* family of today — yet according to the latest statistics such units represent no more than 0.1 per cent of all families. Statistics for end-year 1987 indicated that nuclear families accounted for a fairly low 41.2 per cent of all families (in 1990 52 per cent, including consensual unions); on the other hand, the figure for families with children was 80. Most children are born and live in nuclear families in which at least one of the parents is the child's biological father or mother. At this point, however, it is important to observe that the traditional meaning of the nuclear family has also changed: it is no longer linked the way in which the parents participate in the active labour force (husband provider, wife homemaker), nor does it take account of the sequence of marriages.

Using statistical data we can get different images of families. Table 1 presents one picture of Finnish families by family status and Table 2 another one by family type.

16

Table 1
Finnish population by family status in 1987

Family status	Persons	%
Persons, total	4,879,000	100
Living in families with children under 18 years	2,444,000	50
Married or cohabiting couples	1,118,000	23
Single parents	84,000	2
Children (under and over 18)	1,241,000	25
Living in some other kind of family	2,435,000	34
Married or cohabiting couple with no children	883,000	18
Other: couple or single parent with children over 18	431,000	9
Children over 18 in another family	340,000	7
Single	782,000	16

Source: Saari & Sauli 1991, 46

Table 2
Finnish families by type on 31 December 1987

| | Families | Families with children in all | Type of family | |
			married couple with children	consensual couple with common children
In all	1,244,533	643,993	513,318	32,380
All children common		513,187	486,262	26,925
All children not common				
Common and other children		21,297	15,955	5,342
Only mother's children			5,794	-
Only father's children			902	
Mother's and father's children			372	

Source: Official family statistics, ref. Tolkki-Nikkonen 1990, 107

Zinn (1991) has pointed out that many alternatives which now appear as new are actually variant family patterns that have existed within minority communities for several generations. Presented as new lifestyles of the mainstream, they are in fact the same lifestyles that in the past were deemed pathological, deviant, or unacceptable when observed in minority families. The same applies to new family forms: many of them — such as consensual unions and single-parent families — have long traditions in Finland, but it is only recently that they have been accepted and counted as families.

Cohabitation is a good example. Of all Finnish couples, 16 per cent are cohabiting and about one third of divorced persons live in consensual unions. Around 8 per cent of all families with children are consensual unions. When the man and the woman in a consensual union have no common children, the children in the family are usually the mother's. At the beginning of the 1970s, when cohabitation became more general, about one quarter of married couples in Finland had cohabited before marriage; at that time this was considered an insecure, unconventional, radical, independent and bold solution. By the mid-1980s, almost all married couples had cohabited before marriage; cohabitation is now the rule rather than the exception (Tolkki-Nikkonen 1990).

Second image of families: Process

An examination of the structure of families provides us only with a cross-sectional view. Yet family boundaries change across the family's life course, as do perceptions of who falls within and outside the family system. Rather than concentrating on the family's composition and biological and legal relations, we should indeed consider it from the point of view of the social relations involved and define it as a process: as a system of relations which varies with time and which extends beyond the household unit. Liljeström (1991) suggests that this understanding is best described by the term 'family circle'. Rather than in terms of models or different structures, we can conceptualize the family as temporary, transitory situations. A typical situation is that of extended families after divorce, with the adults living separately and the children orbiting them like satellites. However, this kind of family in which the relationships still work is a new, 'ideal' construction of an after-divorce family. Experiences of joint custody, for instance, have so far not been very good.

Varied images of family

What does the family mean to individuals at different stages of the family life cycle and in different households? In Finland the concept of the family remains fairly nuclearistic. According to some studies made by students (ref. Tolkki-Nikkonen 1990), most people think that the family usually consists of parents and children. There were no major differences in this respect between people at different life stages. Furthermore, it seems that for Finnish people the most important factors which make a family are emotional bonds, joint household and kinship. Students more often referred to kinship; nuclear families underlined the meaning of children; single-parent families mostly mentioned joint household; and reconstructed families emphasized the importance of emotional bonds and marriage. Finnish children usually consider their family as consisting of father, mother and children. People who have experiences of living in different family forms also tend to have broader concepts of the family. Since families are structured around gender and age, women, men, girls and boys do not experience their families in the same way: women, for instance, include more persons in their family than men.

What does the family do to women?

What does the family do for women? What does it do to women? For decades, Finnish women have participated in the active labour force quite extensively, even compared with the other Nordic countries. Statistically, as well as in practice, the 'normal' Finnish family today is a two-earner family. In 1989, 85 per cent of all Finnish mothers were classified as 'economically active', while the corresponding figure for sole mothers was 90 per cent. Only about ten per cent of women are employed on a part-time basis in Finland. Most mothers work full-time, but they also try to find the time for themselves and for their hobbies outside the home. On top of this they try to live up to the traditional model of motherhood and to be a good, devoted mother to their children. There is perhaps no area of family life that is more laden ideologically than the one surrounding the woman's role as mother. The ambivalence between the practices of mothering and the old attitudes towards motherhood makes it extremely difficult for women to strike a reasonable balance between work and home.

On average, Finnish people spent 2 hours 46 minutes a day on housework in 1979: gainfully employed men used 14 hours and women 26 hours a week. Since then there has been a tendency towards greater sharing in household chores. This does not mean that men now spend more time on housework; it means that women use less time than before. Small children in the family significantly increase the women's work load at home; the men are affected to a much lesser extent. In fact, men often add to housework rather than contribute to it (Niemi 1988). There is also a very stable pattern regarding the father's involvement in different tasks, starting with child care. The time spent on child care has indeed increased. This holds true for all the Nordic countries. Doing the laundry, cooking and cleaning are women's work. In this situation domestic labour often becomes an arena for gender struggle. In principle, men stand for gender equality, but only so far as it does not concern themselves.

The myth of family unity has coexisted with a seemingly contradictory belief in individualism. This has been possible because the 'family's interest' has been synonymous with the husband's/father's interest. This conflict between autonomy and the individual's self-development and, on the other hand, family ties is clearly visible in the results of Finnish studies. Young people seem to be afraid of getting married, which is reflected in an ambivalent (Strandell 1984) or even negative (Niemi & Rauste von Wright 1980) attitude towards marriage. At the same time, there is high appreciation for couple relationship (Helve 1987; Niemi 1988; Nurmi 1983). Even this, however, is not without contradictions. For example, young girls who are planning to invest in a job or a career feel that starting a family is in many respects problematic (Nummenmaa & Vanhalakka-Ruoho 1985, 175). The traditional family imposes considerable restrictions on the freedom of its members, particularly for women. The modern family, by contrast, is an arrangement in which independent individuals are primarily devoted to their own development and self-fulfilment; their commitment to the couple relationship and the family is more conditional.

In his study of changing life-values in Finland in 1963-1986, Suhonen (1988, 113) says that there has been progressively less appreciation for security and permanence at the expense of individualistic freedom and self-realization. Women in particular seem to value self-realization, the possibility to do something new and original, more than formerly.

References

Bernandes, Jon (1988), 'Founding the New 'Family Studies'', *The Sociological Review* no 1.

Gubrium, Jaber F. (1987), 'Organizational Embeddedness and Family Life', in Brubaker, Timothy H. (ed.), *Aging, Health and Family*, Sage, Newbury Park.

Helve, Helena (1987), *Nuorten maailmankuva*, Kansalaiskasvatuksen keskus r.y., Tutkimuksia ja selvityksiä 1.

Liljeström, Rita & Kollind, A-K. (1990), *Kärleksliv och föräldrarskap*, Carlssons bokförlag.

Liss, Lora (1987), 'Families and the Law', in Sussman, M.B. & Steinmetz, Susanne K. (eds.), *Handbook of Marriage and the Family*, Plenum Press, New York.

Lorber, Judith & Farrell, Susan A. (eds.) (1991), *The Social Construction of Gender*, Sage, Newbury Park.

Niemi, Iiris (1989), *Ajankäytön muutossuunnat*. Raportti 25.10.1988 sosiaalihallituksen seminaarista Yhteensovittuuko perhe ja työaika? Sosiaalihallituksen raporttisarja Nro 3, Helsinki.

Niemi, Päivi (1988), *Adolescents and the Family. Images and experiences of family life in Finland*, Annales Universitatis Turkuensis, Ser. B - tom 181, Turku.

Niemi, Päivi & Rauste von Wright, Maija-Liisa (1980), *Nuorison ihmis- ja maailmankuva XI. Tyttöjen ja poikien käsityksiä avioliitosta*, Turun yliopisto, Psykologian tutkimuksia 37.

Nummenmaa, Anna-Raija & Vanhalakka-Ruoho, Marjatta (1985), *Toisen sukupuolen ammattiin suuntautuminen. Ammatti, sukupuoli ja työmarkkinat*, Tutkimusprojektin loppuraportti, Työvoimaministeriö, Työvoimapoliittisia tutkimuksia nro 55, Helsinki.

Nurmi, Jari-Erik (1983), *Nuorten tulevaisuuteen suuntautuminen I*, Turun yliopisto, Psykologian tutkimuksia 63.

Saari, Matti & Sauli, Hannele (1990), *Uusperheitä laskemassa*, Hyvinvointikatsaus 4.

Saari, Matti & Sauli, Hannele (1991), *Perheisiin kuuluvat lähes kaikki tai tuskin kukaan*, Hyvinvointikatsaus 2.

Stanley, Liz & Wise, Sue (1983), *Breaking Out: Feminist Consciousness and Feminist Research*, Routledge & Kegan Paul, London.

Suhonen, Pertti (1988), *Suomalaisten arvot ja politiikka*, WSOY, Juva.

Tolkki-Nikkonen, Mirja (1990), *Parisuhde, perhesuhde, olosuhde*, Gaudeamus, Helsinki.

Trost, Jan (1988), 'Conceptualizing the Family', *International Sociology* 3.

Zinn, Maxine Baca (1991), 'Family, feminism, and race in America', in Lorber & Farrell.

2 Female lifestyles and postmodern consciousness

Liisa Knuuti

In this article I describe the process of modernization and its impact on the female lifestyles in Helsinki and its environs. The process of urbanization began relatively late in Finland, but it was extremely rapid and intensive. Today for the first time in history, the majority of the people who live in towns were also born in towns. Finnish women have always worked side by side with men, and a growing number of women is today able to choose a career, if they so wish. Combining a career and family life is quite difficult, however, and many women put off starting a family of their own. In postmodern times new occupations and professions, as well as new values have come about together with the urban lifestyle. In the following, I shall describe the lifestyle and values of the Finnish woman living in an urban environment. I do this by presenting two cases, one focusing on the career, the other on the family.

The female tradition in Finland

In the nineteenth century the new upper and middle classes were profiled according to their wealth, education and lifestyle. As the earlier social identifications changed, the new classes sought to distinguish themselves from the common people. They did this by aping the cultural habits of the European upper classes and that of their own wealthy, yet diminutive nobility. The stage was the home and the private world around it. Status was displayed through property and possessions, as well as lifestyle. While different social classes were distinguished by their level of education and civilization, the changes that occurred in the new middle class were largely based on the woman's work and her role. The spread of education among women affected the status-based ideal of the refined wife. The tradition of the educated housewife still prevails in Finland: the woman should become cultured, but she should not go to work.

The ideal of the woman working for the good of her family already prevailed in the upper class circles by the first half of last century. These women, however, constituted only a very small social group so the ideal cannot be said to have permeated the whole of Finnish society. In Anglo-Saxon studies, the basic assumption seems to be that women first started their families and only then began to participate in working life. This is only partly applicable to the Finnish conditions. In this country most people, men and women alike, participated in production outside the home. In the short period from the end of last century to the 1960s, the idea of the woman as a primary family member became widely accepted.

Women's entry to paid employment was not an outcome of emancipatory struggle, but rather of changes in society. In the old agrarian society men and women were workmates and economically equal, for through their own work women had the opportunity to influence decision-making. This economic equality was based on the high use value of women's work which also met the needs of a simple commodity economy.

The typical bourgeois model of sexual differentiation — the man as the breadwinner, the woman as the wife and mother — has never been so strong in Finland as in the more pronounced class societies of Europe which also experienced industrialization much earlier. The backward Finland needed the women's labour in both industry and agriculture. Moreover, since Finland had no migrant workers, the country needed the women's labour to effect the rapid growth in industry and services that took place after the Second World War.

In 1984 the percentage of employed women in Finland varied from 66 per cent to 77 per cent, while the corresponding figure in the other Western European countries in the mid 1980s was between 33 per cent and 59 per cent. So the Finnish women have always worked hard, creating an image of the strong and hard working woman.

Modernization and lifestyles

Briitta Koskiaho (1986) linked the concept of the 'way of life' to an analysis of the period of cultural criticism in the 1970s. By examining the way of life, researchers wanted to find out how people really live. They used both objective observation and subjective experience. Their main goal was to study individuals as historical beings in their own social and physical environment and through their own set of values.

In his project in 1981, Jeja-Pekka Roos examined the ways of living of the people in the Finnish capital of Helsinki and in the province of North Karelia. The study showed that it is important to understand people's different circumstances and backgrounds, because they lead to a different logic of life. According to Roos, it is important to distinguish between two aspects in the way of life: firstly, the realization of life, including external and internal control of life, and secondly, the basic and open life experiences. Roos examines the way of life through negation and from the standpoint of survival and displacement. He does this by finding out, if there is helplessness, poverty or deprivation (meaning divergent behaviour) in a person's life. Internal control of life may express itself as more or less genuine 'management of one's life'. Genuine inner control is an expression of a person's autonomy.

The special features in a person's way of life are connected to different histories and fortunes of life, manifesting themselves as lifestyles. Here we speak of lifestyles as the way individuals, families and groups of people live in their communities. Koskiaho regards Roos' concept of the way of life in this sense as decisive in the research of different lifestyles. Where the lifestyle is defined by the community, the way of life means the totality in which the lives of community members are divided into functions of everyday life, as well as into thoughts, values, ideals and social morals. Koskiaho, however, sees human beings as individuals who have a will of their own and who want to change the world with their mind. She presumes that the research on lifestyles relates to the subjective concept of goodness in which the role of different views of the world should be taken into account more than before. She thinks that research on lifestyles should try to find out how a person's basic needs can be satisfied in the future. The meaning of work in relation to the use of time and as the basis of material wellbeing will change, which will affect lifestyles. In addition, the opportunities available to a person to change his or her life are still a central problem in the research on wellbeing (Koskiaho 1986, 87-90).

Roos has defined the concept of the way of life in his article in 1990 as follows: The way of life is formed by all those repeated activities which fill a person's everyday life — work, living, leisure and family life. The way of life is often compressed into one dominant feature (food, training, music), but more importantly, the way of life is always a conglomerate of its qualities. The way of life is a wholeness, a certain system, the opposite of the mosaic of separate life activities. Roos uses Pierre Bourdieu's concept of 'habitus' to describe the lifestyles of people. Roos calls habitus the internalized rules of choices. Habitus is a collection of the principles of lifestyles. People can change their way of talking or dressing, but it is not as easy to change one's habitus.

Philosophers, psychologists, economists and other scientists have discussed the issue of lifestyle for a long time. In the Marxist order, lifestyle is a phenomenon primarily determined by an individual's objective position in the production process, that is, in the structure that loosely shapes the values and attitudes and determines the critical life experiences.

Max Weber is more clearly concerned with lifestyle. He uses the term 'status honour'. Status honour is usually expressed as a specific style of life that, above all else, can be expected from those who wish to belong to the particular circle (Dunin-Woyseth 1989, 6). Bearing in mind all our definitions of lifestyle, we should emphasize the last one and call lifestyle a person's pattern of choices or freedom to choose. Lifestyle is a characteristic of a person, a group of people, or society who can afford free choices. Lifestyle thus results from people's values and options. Lifestyle innovation lies in the growing degree of freedom that individuals have in organizing their lives and choosing their lifestyles.

Modernization manifests itself as differentiation on many cultural and economic levels. In its core it is differentiation. It also means that work and leisure are separated from each other. Modern lifestyle means segmentation of different things. Life spheres do not meet (Siurala 1994, 219). Scott Lash (1990) defines postmodernism as de-differentiation. Initially this development emerged in culture where the isolation and the specific nature of different cultural and social actions vanished.

Mike Featherstone (1991) emphasizes the cultural aspect of modernization. He speaks of lifestyles and sees mass consumption as something that has changed into pluralistic postmodern consumption. Featherstone has been influenced by Bourdieu and sees consumption, too, as tied to social class. In his opinion the dominant class of the postmodern city is the new middle class. The members of the new middle class function as the cultural mediators of the commodities and services of symbol production. According to him, this new middle class includes advertising people, TV producers, dealers, journalists, new art workers and new service employees, such as health and other therapists, dieticians, real estate and property consultants, etc. What is essential is how Featherstone defines the consumer society. He no longer approaches it in materialistic terms but rather, by referring to Baudrillard, sees it as a system of giving meanings. The consumption of the postmodern society should therefore be understood in cultural terms. This way the aesthetic aspect of lifestyles and everyday life assume an important role in Featherstone's definitions. According to him, the everyday life of a postmodern urban resident is to a growing extent based on the search for style, latest fashion and experiences. Featherstone also speaks of calculating hedonism, which means that a lifestyle can become a life project.

Thomas Ziehe is another researcher who has studied the way of life and lifestyle in the 1990s (1989). Ziehe bases his cultural analysis on the description of the development of socialization, but his theoretical text can also be applied to the research of lifestyles. Ziehe uses the mythological figure of Narcissus as his central metaphor. He emphasizes the cultural dimension of social modernization and sees it as including lifestyle and the moderni-zation of meanings. This kind of development not only changes the objective reality but also the subjective and internal reality through which we experience realities. Cultural modernization, which in the past was only possible for artists, philosophers and social debators, is everyday life to all of us today.

The disappearance of traditionality in culture presupposes that new forms of knowing emerge, opening up new potentials.

Reflective forms of knowing are spreading. The possibilities of building up one's own personality in an individual way are increasing, but at the same time the demand for even greater individuality is also growing. These possibilities are nothing new, but it is only recently that they have penetrated everyday life and the life of children and young people. A new phenomenon is that 'no future' spontaneity, indulgence, sensuality and immediate satisfaction of needs are making their own demands. Moreover, one has to be able to enjoy life (Ziehe 1989).

Postmodernism, consumer culture

Consumer culture is premised on the expansion of capitalist commodity production which has given rise to a vast accumulation of material culture in the form of consumer goods and sites for purchase and consumption. This has resulted in the growing salience of leisure and consumption activities in contemporary Western societies which, although greeted as leading to greater egalitarianism and individual freedom by some, is regarded by others as increasing the capacity for ideological manipulation and seductive containment of the population from some alternative set of better social relations. The focus here is on the different ways in which people use goods in order to create social bonds or distinctions. There is also the question of the emotional pleasures of consumption, the dreams and desires which become celebrated in the imagery of consumer culture and in the particular sites of consumption which variously generate direct bodily excitement and aesthetic pleasures (Featherstone 1991, 13).

Featherstone refers to Baudrillard who sees postmodern culture as the culture of the consumer society. It may also be possible to claim a consumption logic which points to the socially structured ways in which goods are used to demarcate social relationships. Bourdieu examines the ways goods are used to mark social differences and to act as communicators. In this respect the work of Douglas and Isherwood (1980) is particularly important because of their emphasis on the way in which goods are used to draw the lines of social relationships. Our enjoyment of goods, they argue, is only partly related to their physical consumption and is, in fact, crucially linked to their use as markers. We love sharing the names of goods with others, for example.

For Bourdieu (1984) 'taste classifies and classifies the classifier'. Consumption and lifestyle preferences involve discriminatory judgements which at the same time identify and render classifiable our own particular taste to others. Particular constellations of taste, consumption preferences and lifestyle practices are associated with specific occupations and class fractions, making it possible to map out the universe of taste and lifestyle with its structured opposition and finely graded distinctions which operate within a particular society at a particular point in history. In this context knowledge becomes important: knowledge of new goods, their social and cultural value and how to use them appropriately. This is particularly the case with aspiring groups who adopt a learning mode towards consumption and the cultivation of a lifestyle. Bourdieu reminds us of his concept of symbolic capital, which means the knowledge of the consumption of the right goods (Featherstone 1991, 18).

Mary Douglas argues that 'to the consumers themselves, consumption is less like a pleasure for its own sake and more like pleasurable fulfilment of social duties' (Douglas 1982).

Lash sees modernization as culminating in cities. According to him, modernism would not even have come about without cities, or modernization needed urbanization in which to develop (Lash 1990, 31). Georg Simmel, too, refers to metropolitan cities which to him are the only places where a modern lifestyle can develop.

For the first time in history most young Finns living in the 1990s were born in cities. In the 1950s only 20 per cent of Finnish people were living in towns, but in the 1990s the corresponding figure is about 70 per cent. A major rural-urban migration took place in the 1960s and the 1970s. At that time many people moved from the north of the country to southern Finland. Many new housing areas were built following functionalist architectural principles. In the beginning people disliked them and had a great desire to move back to the countryside. The new generation in Finland no longer has such direct connections to the countryside. They are the ones who should create the new urban culture.

The lifestyle of women in the Scandinavian countries

The Danish ethnologist Thomas Hojrup's model of lifestyle (1992) is constructed of existential conditions which include economical, political, ideological and juridical conditions — all of which dominate a family's form of livelihood. The form of livelihood is tied to the position of the production structure. Examining a family's lifestyle means observing how the social classes develop self-constructed routines in their everyday life. The concept of lifestyle includes both cognitive and material aspects. The cognitive aspect refers to the way a person interprets his or her daily mundane activities. It includes the individual's view of life, position in society, values, norms and social relations, ideal of family life, local social life, ideas of right and wrong, duties and rights. Højrup identifies the lifestyles of the different conditions: entrepreneur, wage earner and careerist. The two latter are common lifestyles among women in the Scandinavian countries.

The Swedish Tora Friberg (1992) has examined the differences between the lifestyles of two women (one is a wage earner, the other a careerist) with the help of time geography. Her examples were Mia, a day nursery assistant, and Anita, a medical doctor. Friberg states that women try to avoid a lifestyle which is too connected with their career, because due to the lack of time and the difficulties in organizing everyday chores they regard that kind of lifestyle too demanding and stressful. This is because women, unlike men, do not have the support of their family while building their career. It is not self-evident that a woman's ambition is to become a director. Usually women strive to become specialists by deepening their knowledge of the subject. They are prepared to work overtime and sacrifice parts of their leisure time. The whole personality of such women is absorbed by their work and that is why they have a great need to develop themselves further. They do not have the patience to wait until their children have grown up. They are ambitious enough to keep on studying and are prepared to take on more demanding tasks in their profession. They do not want the role of the housewife to dominate their life. This does not mean, however, that they do not pay any attention to their children. They are very ambitious about spending their time with their children and developing them. The career women's lack of time can be seen in that they do not do much housework but, instead, spend their spare time playing with their children. A career woman cannot wait for her children to grow up, she must have everything here and now.

The lifestyle of a wage earner is completely different. For her, working is a way to earn money which in turn makes it possible for her to lead a satisfying life outside the working hours. The women who live the life of a wage earner have a meagre schooling: they work in factories, hospitals and shops. Wage earner women clearly outnumber career women.

The features of urban lifestyles concentrate on experiencing the city, moving in the city, acting in the city and encountering the city. The themes of the interviews made in the Helsinki Metropolitan Area in the early 1990s were: structure of everyday life, social interaction, consciousness, values, hobbies, ways of consumption and demands (Knuuti 1992).

In the following I shall describe the lifestyles of two women. One of them represents the new middle class and is a dealer by profession. Her work is independent, she need not follow ordinary working hours, she has a degree in business administration, and she must take quite big risks in her work. Her salary depends on her success in her job. She has a possibility of advancement in her career. The other woman is an office secretary. Her work is dependent in nature, she has had no special education for her work, and her working hours are regular. Her chances of advancing in her career are very small indeed. She belongs to the lower middle class.

Here we may use Friberg's concepts of career lifestyle and wage earner lifestyle. The former implies that the woman makes use of her free time, too, to ensure success in her job. She also brings work home, in one way or another. Wage earner lifestyle, on the other hand, means that work ensures an income which, in turn, makes it possible to live a real life outside the working hours (Friberg 1992, 60-61).

Ulrich Beck (1986) observes the development of the welfare state which has led to a situation in which everyone has more of material good, in a collective sense. This in turn leads to the 'lift-effect'. Consequently, as everyone has gained more of the good, the sub-cultures of social classes, class identities and class formations have became thinner or have dissolved. The value system of individualism is based on a new kind of ethic: your most important duty is to yourself. As a result of the lift-effect and the rise of individualism, everyone now has more options to choose from than ever before. You can choose your own lifestyle.

In the following discussion I examine values from the viewpoint of social psychology, using the definition developed by Shalom Schwartz (Schwartz 1992). Values are concepts or beliefs which have to do with the desired outcomes or behaviour. Values exceed concrete situations and guide our choices and judgements. In addition, values are organized according to their relative importance. Schwartz's value theory is based on empirical studies made in 20 countries.

Riitta, 29, office secretary from Espoo

Riitta represents the lifestyle of a wage earner. For her working is a source of income which gives her the possibility to live a real life in her spare time. Work gives her a salary and a group of friends. Spare time provides her with an identity. For a woman this means a close connection to housework. This is the greatest difference compared to the lifestyle of a career woman. Riitta works as an office assistant in a small civil service department in Espoo. She has a husband and one child. They live in a modern terraced house 20 kilometres away from the centre of Helsinki. She gives a great deal of attention to the wellbeing of her child and the family. The skeleton of her daily life is formed by little mundane routines which take up most of her time.

As is usual in the capital region, the distance between home and office is quite long. Because of the high prices of housing Riitta has had to buy a flat far away from the centre of the city. Even though her husband takes the child to the day care, Riitta does not usually have much free time. Work, daily shopping, housework and care of the child take up a lion's share of Riitta's day. She wakes up at six o'clock in the morning and from then on her schedule is very busy and stress-inducing. Riitta gets up twenty minutes before the rest of the family to have at least a little moment to herself. The other free moment of the day for her is the lunch hour at work during which she can run her own errands. Her daily schedule is very busy and systematic. Housework takes up a large part of her day. Her hobbies have to do with keeping fit: gymnastics, aerobics, and slalom in the winter. In her free time Riitta does nothing that would have any connection to her work.

Inner harmony and the sense of belonging are very important values to her. Real friendship, security of the family and meaningfulness of life are perhaps the most important values to her. Riitta does not think that an exciting life is something she should look for. She thinks exciting things just happen and they will happen to her, too, in due course. Riitta does not appreciate an ascetic lifestyle, though. In her opinion that kind of lifestyle restricts a person far too much. She is not interested in reaching power or authority in society. She would be prepared to sacrifice something to prevent environmental catastrophes from happening. In her daily activities she likes to take ecological effects into account. However, she is not prepared to go as far as chain herself on to trees or join a group of environmentalists.

The meaningfulness of life is of great value to her. To this she adds self-respect, which is important at home, as well as among friends and in the office. Friends mean a lot to her. She has many friends and spends as much of her time with them as her family allows. Her friends do not work in the same office. When she is out with her friends, her husband looks after the child.

In her own opinion Riitta is not a believer, even though some traditions like going to church at Christmas and on other religious holidays are important to her. Riitta does not want to live on her own or to lead an exciting life: she rather wants to take care of others and do things together with other people. Honesty and health are also important issues to her. Making her way upwards in the office and advancing in her career do not mean much to her. Riitta has accepted the traditional role of woman even though she goes to work. She does the housework together with her husband. As it takes up so much of their time, one could say that family is the most important hobby for both of them. Friends and relatives come close to the family.

Even though Riitta has to use a large part of her salary to pay back the loan she took to buy the flat, she still enjoys spending money and wants to do so. The lack of money does not prevent her from going from shop to shop and looking for possible things to buy — it gives her great pleasure just to see what the shops are displaying each month. Riitta says that even though, due to her financial circumstances, she has to save money, she still can consume. She does not favour any particular product names and thinks that buying Finnish products is not important in itself. Only when it comes to jeans, she always buys the same brand. Usually she wears jeans and sweaters; she does not think much of fancy clothes. She does not have much time for reading, even though she always tries to read a few pages of a novel or a magazine before falling asleep at night.

In Finland women have always worked outside the home and they are quite independent compared to women in many other countries. Because of economical independence it is quite easy for a woman to devote her life to herself. If a woman is successful in her work, she is also respected as an independent woman. It is therefore possible for a woman to live an independent life, free from the paralyzing mundane chores, if she wants to. She can enjoy life without a worry in the world. But like Riitta, women still have to take care of their children and drive them to the day care in the morning and back home after work. After an eight-hour working day women must still do the housework. Nowadays a woman can stay at home for three years after childbirth to look after her children, and her job will still be there for her when she returns to work. This is not possible, however, if a woman wants to have a brilliant career as well. Career women do not want to become housewives, for they find that kind of life boring. Besides, they would lose their place in society. Riitta thinks differently. She was at home for three years, when her daughter was a baby.

Leena, 31, currency dealer from Helsinki

Leena does not exist as an individual. She is a fictitious prototype of a typical single urban woman and her values and ways of action are derived from five different interviews with young urban females. Leena's parents belong to the lower middle class and have lived in Helsinki all their life. Thirty years ago they graduated from a college.

Leena works in a large bank as a currency dealer, buying and selling money.

The lifestyle of a young independent woman mostly centres around herself and her job. She can lead an almost 'heroic life' — she can concentrate on succeeding in her profession, taking care of her looks and having fun. Her everyday life is not filled with routines or boring domestic tasks. Leena is not married and even though she has a boyfriend, she does not live with him but lives alone in a small flat in the centre of Helsinki. She does not have to cook daily, because she can have lunch in the bank cafeteria. She does not have to buy groceries every day or start another working day as soon as she gets home. She likes to go out with her friends to have a beer or two after work. She only cooks at weekends, together with her friends. They usually watch video tapes and sometimes play squash or go swimming. She does not go in for sports much, though. She concentrates on being good at her profession, and she tries continuously to acquire skills that might prove useful in her job.

Health plays a central part in her set of values. She is very anxious about her health, even though she has never been seriously ill. Because of the increasing pollution of the environment, she is afraid of all sorts of bacteria and unknown diseases. Unlike real health freaks, however, she does not resort to eating sprouts or other similar things. If something alarming should happen to her health, she believes that oatmeal porridge could bring about the cure.

She has no special feelings for the sick and the poor and thinks it is not her responsibility to help them. She does not like to make sacrifices. She wants to make it on her own and look after herself only — if people do not manage on their own, it is their own problem. The issues of the Third World do not concern her at all.

Environmental issues do not interest her so much that she would be prepared to give something up for them. She is only concerned about those things that make her own life more difficult. She does not want to go to the extreme to save our daily environment.

Safety rates very high in her set of values, as do traditions. She does not care much for a bohemian lifestyle or bad behavior. She hopes that when she eventually decides to have a family, they could lead a quiet family life. She has a boyfriend, and she likes intimate relationships and tenderness, but she despises the mundane routines so much that she is not prepared to tie herself for good just yet. She hates the idea of having to drag her children to day care and back home every day, before and after work. Some time ago a bachelor girl in her thirties was not respected, but nowadays there is no social pressure like that. In Finland an independent single woman can be respected, if she has a good and highly paid job. Very few people can afford a car and a flat at the age of 25 — Leena had them both and is proud of it.

35

Clothes and a personal style are very important to Leena. She is very conscious of the designers whose clothes she wears and has many of her clothes specially made. She gets many of her fashion ideas from international magazines and she buys loads of clothes when travelling abroad. There are some Finnish clothes that she cannot wear because she does not like the designer. If people saw her wearing them, they could get a wrong image of her. She is very conscious of what things suit her style and are 'in'. There are some expensive clothes by Finnish designers that she likes and she also buys furniture by Artek and china by Arabia, both renowned for their high quality products. She knows that she has to be very elegant because of her job. She often meets foreigners and she has to look presentable.

Leena often dines in expensive restaurants with her business guests, but she always meets her friends in the same restaurant. She can always get in there, even if the place is full. She likes her urban living environment in the very centre of Helsinki. She often walks around the city checking out shops, visits the marketplace and the new shopping centres. Money and consuming are the most important things in her life. With regard to cultural activities, Leena is a very average person. She likes her films to be entertaining and undemanding and does not care much for the theatre or the opera. She watches TV a lot and listens to pop music programmes on the radio. She does not read much.

The dark side of the career lifestyle reveals indifference to others and to the environment, a kind of morally accepted, modern selfishness. Everyone knows that only a few can live their life this way. You must have a good education and a lot of know-how — only they can ensure you a good place in the business world. This kind of life is only possible in times of flourishing economy. Something will change during a recession, but no one knows what will happen.

For now Leena can lead a heroic life. Life is an adventure to her, full of possibilities and happy experiences. But a self-devoted woman must change her lifestyle, if she wants to have children. In today's Finland a woman can devote her life to being a successful bachelor girl and hardly anyone will disapprove. In fact, women are at present quite visible in most professions.

Postmodern lifestyle and the young women

Can one talk of postmodern consciousness in Leena's case? In some ways, yes. Does postmodernism mean that 'everything smelts into the air' (Berman 1982)? Or is it the current way of asking questions, a new kind of thinking or consciousness which manifests itself in architecture, art, literature, philosophy, and in the lifestyles of people, in everything that was happening in the late eighties.

The postmodern mood means that when the human being breaks down the taboos and reveals the artificial, it is impossible to find the real ego, a true individual. A new surface will emerge, endlessly. The postmodern mood knows that, and so he or she will dress the conscious with the artificial. And he or she also knows that after one limit there will be another, and he or she has to live on the limit, while no one knows what will happen tomorrow. But the feeling of irony and paradox gives us the possibility to live in this age, which is full of threats and catastrophes.

We can note an elective affinity between postmodernist culture and bourgeois identity. Here we can draw on Bourdieu's notion of the 'habitus'. The habitus describes the lifestyles of people. The habitus means the internalized rules of choices. It is like a collection of the principles of lifestyles. People change their way of talking or dressing, but it is not easy to change your habitus. We can understand the habitus, and thus identity, in terms of Durkheim's conscience collective, which itself has two components: (1) the component of the 'group', which defines identity in terms of in-group and out-group, in terms of the boundaries between the individual or collective actor and those different from, and often standing in opposition to, the individual or collective actor; (2) the component of classification. Part of our identity is determined by how we classify. We classify 20 individuals into genders, age groups, ethnicities, social classes and status groups. To classify is necessarily at the same time to evaluate, to make invidious distinctions. Different social classes and class fractions, observes Bourdieu, have different systems of classifications. New, post-industrial middle classes, with their bases in the media, higher education, finance, advertising, merchandising, and international exchanges provide an audience for postmodern culture. The populism and image-centredness of postmodernism is more appealing to the new groupings than to the old elite.

Postmodern culture can thus be seen as a set of symbols and legitimation which promote the ideal interests of this post-industrial bourgeoisie. It is partly constitutive of identity for this grouping (Lash 1990, 19-20).

Powerful hedonism and the need to live for oneself, having fun and consuming are parts of the postmodern lifestyle. Both Leena and Riitta, however, are also quite traditional in the way they respect safety and family ties. In a way they are conservative.

Leena is not postmodernistic in an artistic way. Instead, she rather represents the new Finnish middle class. What is new is that now a woman, too, has a chance to live alone and be free, at least up to the point when she has children. For Leena, making everyday life aesthetic is part of her lifestyle.

Can one talk of postmodern consciousness in Riitta's case? Riitta is a very traditional woman, a real housewife. But she, too, is more independent than the earlier generations of women have been. Her lifestyle is very systematic and filled with programme. Consumption gives her a sense of liberty. Actually Riitta is very modernistic. So we can say that postmodern consciousness is seen in the lifestyles of the postindustrial middle classes, but the majority is still living in the modernistic style.

The economic recession hit Finland in the early 1990s. Its impact began to be felt only after the above interviews had been made. So far the recession, or in fact depression, has not had too great an effect on the lives of those who have managed to hold on to their jobs. Actual or threatening unemployment has, however, influenced people's ways of consumption: they are much more economical now. Uncertainty has also resulted in a great interest in psychological matters. Philosophy, for example, is extremely popular these days. People now have to depend on more temporary employment or they have to gain their livelihood from a number of different sources. This demands greater flexibility and tolerance of uncertainty and diffusion, that is, a 'postmodern' attitude towards life.

References

Beck, Ulrich (1986), *Risikogesellschaft. Auf dem Weg zum Anderen Moderne*, Surkamp, Frankfurt am Main.

Berman, Marshall (1982), *All That is Solid Smelts into Air*, Simon Schuster, New York.

Bourdieu, Pierre (1984), *Distinction, a Social Critique of the Judgement of Task*, Routledge & Kegan Paul, London.

Douglas, Mary, Isherwood Baron (1982), *The Effect of Modernization on Religious Change*, Daedalus.

Dunin-Woyseth, Halina (1989), *Changing Lifestyles versus Urban Built Form*, Oslo School of Architecture, Paper in AESOP Third Annual Congress: Planning Together in Europe, Tours.

Featherstone, Mike (1991), *Consumer Culture & Postmodernism*, SAGE Publications, London, Newbury Park, New Delhi.

Friberg, Tora (1992), Tidsgeografin synliggör livsformernas praxis, *Nordic Journal of Architectural Research* No 1/1992, Föreningen för Arkitekturforskningen.

Højrup, Thomas (1992), Om den strukturelle livsformsanalysen, *Nordic Journal of Architectural Research* No 1/1992, Föreningen för Arkitekturforskningen.

Ilmonen, Mervi (1991), *Elämää betonissa*, Nuorisoasuntoliitto, Helsinki.

Koskiaho, Briitta (1986), *Yhteiskunnan muutos ja sosiaalipolitiikka*, Tammi, Helsinki.

Koskiaho, Briitta (1990), *Ohi, läpi ja reunojen yli*, Gaudeamus. Helsinki.

Knuuti, Liisa (1992), Postmodernism and Urban Lifestyle in Finland, *Nordic Journal of Architectural Research* No 1/1992, Föreningen för Arkitekturforskningen.

Lash, Scott (1990), *Sociology of Postmodernism*, Routledge, London and New York.

Pohls, Maritta (1990), 'Women's Work in Finland 1870-1940', in Manninen, Merja and Setälä, Päivi (eds), *The Lady with the Bow. The Story of Finnish Women*, Otava, Keuruu.

Roos, Jeja-Pekka (1981), Elämäntapojen tyypeistä elämäkertojen valossa, *Sosiologia* No 4/1981.

Roos, Jeja-Pekka (1981), Elämäntapojen tyypeistä elämäkertojen valossa, *Sosiologia* No 4/1981. Westermarck-seura.

Roos, Jeja-Pekka (1987), *Suomalainen elämä. Tutkimus tavallisten suomalaisten elämäkerroista*, Suomalaisen kirjallisuuden seura, Helsinki.

Roos, Jeja Pekka (1990), Suomalaisen elämäntavan muutokset, article in Riihinen, Olavi (ed.), *Suomi 2017*, Gummerus, Jyväskylä.

Sayers, Andrew (1984), *Method in Social Science. A Realist Approach*, Hutchinson, London.

Schwartz, Shalom (1992), 'Universals in the Content and Structure of Values: Theoretical Advances and Empirical Tests in 20 Countries', in Zanna, Mark P. (ed.), *Experimental Social Psychology*, Academic Press, San Diego, New York, Boston, London, Sydney, Tokyo, Toronto.

Siurala, Lasse (1994), *Nuoriso-ongelmat modernisaatioperspektiivissä*, Helsingin kaupungin tietokeskuksen tutkimuksia 3, Helsinki 1994.

Wärneryd, Olof (1990), *Bäcklund, Ann-Karin, Löfgren, Anders: Effects of Changing Lifestyles on Urban Growth in Sweden*, Department of Social and Economic Geography, Lund University, Lund.

Ziehe, Thomas (1989), *Kulturanalyser. Ungdom, utbildning, modernitet*, Essäer sammanställda av Johan Fornäs och Joachim Retzlaff i samarbete med författaren, Symposion Bokförlag, Stockholm.

3 Retired female textile workers – life and housing

Maija-Liisa Pättiniemi

Introduction

Mechanized manufacturing industry in Finland is about one hundred and fifty years old. In 1840 there were forty factories, excluding sawmills and ironworks, each having over ten employees. Only two of these were modern mechanized factories, the Finlayson cotton mill in Tampere in central Finland and the Fiskars engineering works in the municipality of Pohja, near the south coast (Kanerva 1946, 335). Large-scale mechanical industry developed quite late in Finland, but its growth was fairly rapid. Cotton industry was established in the 1820s.

Industrialization required a large work force which was brought into towns from the countryside. The towns were not prepared for the extent of rural-urban migration which took place. As a result, the living conditions were poor. Like in England, women and children formed the majority of the factory work force as their labour could be bought at a cheaper rate than that of men.

Industrialization brought along prosperity. Yet, at the turn of the century Finland still remained a poor agricultural country. Only one eighth of the Finnish population lived in towns. Tampere became an industrial 'island' in the poor agrarian society. The workers who moved to the town experienced industrialization as a good thing (Haapala 1986, 385).

In the 1920s, Tampere was a small town by international standards. Its population was 41,500, of which 17,200 were men and 24,300 women. This gender bias in the structure of population resulted from the fact that Tampere was mostly a textile town, and like in many other countries, the textile industry favoured female employees. The Finlayson mill in Tampere at the turn of the century employed young, unmarried women who had moved from the countryside. However, Tampere became an exceptional town and acquired features which made it distinct from all other industrial towns and regions. The Finlayson factory had formed an independent, closed community characterized by unusual corporate spirit. Although the Finlayson closed community structure was to dissolve, the spirit of 'Finlaysonism' lived on well into the late 20th century and continued to influence the lives of its former employees.

In this article I will examine the life and housing careers of the former female Finlayson factory workers. The article is based on a my earlier study (Pättiniemi 1989) which examines life history data, collected from 18 female workers. Their life histories were examined from the standpoint of their own experiences and how they themselves defined the status and role of 'the cotton girls' in society. On the basis of their life histories it is possible to analyse the information on their past in different age periods, as well as on their lives at present.

Finlayson cotton mill

In 1820, a Scotsman called James Finlayson founded an engineering works on the bank of the Tammerkoski Rapids in Tampere. He manufactured machines for his own cotton mill founded in 1827. When Finlayson returned to Scotland and sold the mill in 1835, there were already 500 spindles in operation (Haapala 1986, 24). The cotton mill expanded rapidly. In 1850 there were 1,000 employees, and the mill soon became the largest industrial plant in Finland and all the Nordic countries. Tampere became the centre of textile industry, 'the Manchester of Finland'. After 1850 other mechanized industries followed, such as a paper mill and another engineering works, a linen mill and a textile mill.

In the 1840s the Finlayson factory was the largest employer in Tampere. As Rasila (1984, 39-40) points out, it was like 'a state inside the town'. In its own clearly defined area the factory could do as it pleased. The municipality of Tampere had no rights or

42

authority in the area. The cotton mill had its own citizens who felt they 'belonged', who were 'Finlayson folks' (Rasila 1984, 39-40).

In 1840 the factory began to acquire land in order to provide housing for its employees. In the 1850s the first dwellings with a common kitchen were built. The factory had to build its own accommodation, if it was to attract people from the countryside. At the turn of the century the factory owned 743 rooms, housing 1,825 workers and their family members (Haapala 1986, 65). The dwellings in which one kitchen was shared by several households became characteristic of Tampere workers' housing in general, and other factories began to follow the example of Finlayson.

In the 1840s the factory and its surroundings were declared an independent church parish. It had its own school, orphanage, fire-brigade, two policemen and, in 1860, its own hospital, the first in Tampere (Rasila 1984, 36-37).

In the 19th century cotton industry became Tampere's main source of livelihood. Besides introducing electric light — as the first in Europe in 1882 — the factory adopted the vision of a brighter future for the poor people of Tampere and its surrounding countryside.

The effects of the rapid industrialization caused some anxiety within the Finnish society. The static world picture of the old agricultural society began to falter, when the labour movement was established, importing new ideas from other industrialized countries. The spread of industrialization began to slacken off as political anxiety increased and international economic fluctuations occurred. The growth of Tampere as a town can largely be traced through the development of the cotton mill. By 1910, however, violent economic and social changes affected Tampere and the Finlayson factory (Rasila 1984, 42). Tampere had been transformed from a village of factories into a real industrial town.

In 1900, the number of factory workers in Tampere was 10,000. Of these workers 68 per cent were employed in textile industry. Every third resident thus worked in a factory and every sixth resident in a textile mill, and half of them, over 3,000 workers, at Finlayson. The textile industry work force consisted mainly of young, unmarried women. Tampere became a famous centre of female factory workers. In 1920, women accounted for 54.8 per cent of the factory work force (Haapala 1986, 34-38). In Tampere the number of female factory workers was one and a half times higher than anywhere in Finland. To a certain degree, textile industry also employed children over 12 years. Women and children were cheap labour force. Their work involved tasks usually associated with women's domestic labour, light handiness (Hemmilä 1981, 48). That gave women and children the qualifications to work with machines (Haapala 1986, 50). Their work in textile industry was governed by machines. The Finlayson factory workers came from the surrounding countryside. They represented the poorest sector of the Finnish society (Alanen & Haapala 1979, 5).

The political tension and economic decline in the early part of this century decreased the number of factory workers and threatened their economic situation and security in Finland. It did not, however, affect the numbers employed by Finlayson. The depression of the 1930s hit Finlayson, too, reducing the work force by 700 persons. By 1935 the work force again increased to 3,000, of which 2,250 were women. During the Second World War the number of female workers decreased to 1,040 (total work force 1,400). In 1945 the number of workers began to increase, and in 1950 employment numbers peaked at 2,650, after which the work force began to decline, steadily and permanently.

The life careers of the Finlayson female workers in the light of their life histories

The Finlayson workers employed in the early decades of this century are now retired. During their working life the women experienced politically turbulent and economically unstable times. Their retirement took place just before the catastrophic decline in industrial employment in the 1970s.

When interviewing elderly informants, the life history approach is particularly useful. It is literally history born at present. However, one has to be aware of the unconscious selection process which takes place, when the informants recall their memories and experiences. 'An individual has to choose the most essential events.' (Alasuutari 1986, 9-10.)

Life history cannot be regarded as an objective truth about what has happened in an individual's life. Instead, it must be understood as a possibility to examine, how an individual sees his or her past life. The autobiography reflects the narrator's world picture, how he or she identifies and understands his or her own life experiences.

When autobiographies are used in a sociological or historical study, it is essential to try to check their reality with the help of other sources: reference function. Although, as J.P. Roos has noted in his autobiographical study 'The Finnish Life' (Suomalainen elämä), life stories and autobiographies are unique accounts, but they do follow fairly closely the official historical time scale. It is also important to remember that the informant's meanings are his or her own interpretations or opinions of events. The estimating function gives rise to a subjective truth; the authenticity of individual meanings. This does not lend itself easily to objective verification (Saarenheimo 1988, 265). The validity problem has been clearly recognized within the social sciences. Bertaux (1981), for example, has discussed this problem in a study which examined the social structures of the bakers' profession. He illustrated 'the snowball technique': fifteen life histories formed a picture of the bakers' social structure, while twenty-five life histories saturated that picture.

In the life history accounts given by the female workers, there were certain similarities. Certain events or periods were shared by all informants — wars, shortages and the establishment of the welfare state were recurring themes. Indeed, given such information, the women seem to form a fairly homogeneous social group whose life experiences are similar.

Resources for life provided by the rural community

The informants I interviewed were born between the years 1893 and 1913. Most had come to Tampere from the economically exposed areas of the countryside, from small farming families. A few came from factory workers' families who were already living in the town. As the life histories between informants of rural or urban origin did not differ significantly, I shall focus on the informants born in the countryside.

Childhood At the turn of the century Finland was still very much an agricultural country. In 1920 only 13 per cent of the population gained their living from industry and building, while 70 per cent still obtained their livelihood from agriculture. The rural society was based on a hierarchical and static social structure in which everyone knew his or her place. Patriarchal relations prevailed in the small farmhouse. The father was the head of the household and discipline was strict. Children were socialized at an early age into working hard. Everyday life was touched by material poverty. The farmhouse was usually very small, consisting of a kitchen and only one other room. People lived a life of the bare minimum, meeting their subsistence needs by cultivating a small potato patch. In most households the father had to take on logging work to make ends meet. Although people did not starve, food was never in abundance. Clothes shortages were common, with children having to take turns to wear a pair of shoes. The mothers were in charge of domestic duties. This included the care of livestock and any outbuildings. The female members of the household did not like to be idle. Needlework filled all spare time. The children worked alongside their mothers. The older children were often left in charge of the younger ones. Schooling was frequently neglected. Most children only managed to attend school for four years, the minimum time required to get through elementary school.

Childhood focused on action and work. Family members tended to stay in the background except for one or the other of the parents who had been particularly strict. This was usually the father, reflecting the traditional patriarchal way of life in the countryside.

The material poverty did not really affect the children. It was seen as a part of life.[1] Changes in human relationships did, however, affect the informants' childhood in significant ways. Most of them clearly remembered events such as the death of a family member.

Most of the informants mentioned the Civil War of 1917, as well as Finland's subsequent independence from Russia. Most probably their fathers had been taken away from the household, which had meant that some of the girls, at the early age of only 10 years, had had to go and work as maids away from their homes.

Adulthood in the urban community

Working life The informants had already been taught the value of hard work, obedience and scanty living at home. Because they had had little schooling, factory work was the only opportunity available to them. Some had, however, worked as maids before

46

starting at Finlayson's. As young girls they started work at fifteen years. Until 1917 they worked a ten-hour day. Some had started work as young as twelve; they had only been permitted to work for half a day, however, the rest of the day being spent at Finlayson's school. Although the work was hard, most had been anxious to gain employment. Getting a job at the factory was quite easy: a relative or a friend could inquire on their behalf or they could go to the gate and ask for a work place themselves. When they started work, they were given a fortnight's apprenticeship before being allowed to work on the machines. Girls who had started work before fifteen years of age were allowed to go straight to the machines on their fifteenth birthday.

It is interesting to note how the informants identified particular life stages. For most, starting work signified adulthood, partly because it meant leaving home. This supports Tolkki-Nikkonen's (1985, 12) idea that adulthood or indeed any other life stage, is perceived to begin, when a significant social event or landmark is passed.[2] However, if Tolkki-Nikkonen's idea that starting work signifies adulthood is to be taken at face value, then some of the girls reached adulthood at the age of twelve. As Alasuutari (1986, 31) points out, these girls were socially forced into adulthood.

Freed from the discipline and severity of countrylife, coupled with the money they earned at the mill, the young women were able to enjoy a period of youth. This can be identified as a distinct life stage, i.e. unmarried adulthood. The informants had fond memories of going to the theatre, a dance and the cinema. Earlier they had not had any money or possibilities to enjoy entertainments. The money was neither much nor enough to buy new clothes, but they utilized their needlework skills to brighten up their worn-out clothes. As young women, they valued their newly found freedom and income.

In 1920 only 37 per cent of the female workers were married as compared to 87 per cent of the male work force. Almost invariably the cotton girls were single. The reason was not only their youth or the shortage of men, but staying single was a conscious choice for them. They wanted to live unmarried (Hemmilä 1981, 13). In Tampere the cotton girls were famous for their single status which in part was due to the much higher proportion of women than men in the town, characteristic of the structure of population in Tampere even today. There are many more older women (former cotton girls) than older men. Half of the informants did, however, marry. Dance halls were the main arena for meeting a future husband.

After the girls got married, their family life became established. The women did not really talk about the everyday occurrences of family life or its relationships; they rather talked about significant happenings, such as divorce or widowhood. Divorce was spoken of as a particularly traumatic event. It was rare in the countryside, so the women had no childhood experiences to refer to. 'Happiness' was not considered an important factor in a successful marriage, for in the countryside marriage had been seen as an economic partnership or a work relationship (Ahponen & Järvelä 1983, 234). Divorce was quite rare in towns in the 1920s and 1930s, and represented an economic risk for most women. Although social support was available, the social stigma attached to divorce was so great that most women persevered within a bad marriage.

Unmarried women did not feel the need to get married for economic reasons, since employment at the factory appeared to be secure. Their life circumstances, however, changed somewhat, as they had to care for their elderly parents and relatives. At this time the state assumed little responsibility for elderly people, so the burden was on younger female relatives. Women were expected to care for children as well as other family members without questioning this expansion of their domestic duties.

Work in the mill was both heavy and hectic. Dust in particular was a problem and forced every fourth woman to change her job from spinner to weaver or to stock worker. Despite the disadvantages of factory work, only one woman left the factory, and this was not because of the bad conditions, but she had found a better paid job in a knitwear factory. Most of the informants said they had enjoyed their time at the factory and that it had brought them some kind of job satisfaction. Socializing with the other workers usually took place outside the working hours. At work the women did not even have time to eat, let alone chat. The mill operated under a quota system: wages were related to the amount of work the women did. In general, women's wages were lower than those of male workers at Finlayson's. On average, the women earned one third less than the men. In the industrial sector as a whole, women earned 50 per cent less than men in 1928 (Hemmilä 1981, 32). Although the wages were too low to lead to a significant rise in the standard of living compared to life in the countryside, the women were still relatively better off. They had expected no dramatic rise in their standard of living and were satisfied with smallness, a value they had carried with them from their rural childhood.

The women felt inferior not only to the factory foremen, but to male workers in general. The factory was a production unit with very clear subordinate and hierarchical relationships. Everyone knew his or her place. There was a clear gender based division of labour; men carried out the physically more demanding tasks, but they also occupied the more important (in terms of status and income) managerial roles. Patriarchal values, instilled during childhood, prevented the women from standing up for their rights.

The economic depression of the 1930s and the war years made it more difficult for the women to earn their livelihood. Most of the women managed to meet subsistence needs and to avoid unemployment, however. Finlayson's remained a particularly secure employer. In times of economic depression the women fared slightly better than the men, as the demand for female workers remained somewhat higher. Shortages in raw material meant a reduction in the number of working hours and in wages. This, alongside the introduction of rationing in the war years, reduced the women's consumption levels to a bare minimum. Clothes and foodstuffs in particular were in short supply. The women did not starve, however, since they were able to gain essential supplies from their rural homes or even on the black market.

The informants were employed at Finlayson's for about 32 years. They thought of themselves as 'loyal and truthful' to their employer. For example, none of the women were ever involved in strike action. This loyalty can be partly explained by the fact that the mill became to mean something more to them than just a place of work. It influenced every part of the women's lives, especially amongst unmarried employees. The mill and its community became almost like a substitute family for them. It provided not only housing but also the setting for the community where its members had a strong sense of common identity and belonging. These women belong to the first generation of the present society, 'the generation of war and shortage' (Roos 1987). They brought with them old traditional paternalistic and patriarchal ideologies from the countryside. This was reflected in the gender division and inequality in the work place, as well as in the moral and ethical

49

values of Finlaysonism. Work became the means of achieving citizenship.

Retirement. Because most of the women had centred their lives around the mill, one might have expected that retirement would have been a particularly traumatic event for them and would have meant giving up their work, as well as their sense of 'belonging' to society or the community (Koskiaho 1986, 158-161). Gothoni (1987) and Forss (1982) have found that retirement often leads to 'dissatisfaction' with life. However, they point out that the quality of the retirement years depends on the earlier work circumstances and the existing domestic arrangements.

In the case of the Finlayson workers, the women who were interviewed did not find retirement a problem. Half of the women received early retirement due to asthma caused by the high dust levels in the mill. After a short period of adjustment most of the women came to enjoy their retirement. They were not only glad to escape the hard work involved in factory employment, but also, the retirement years meant that they no longer had a family to care for.

Retirement also signified a decrease in household income. This reduced the women's 'consumption capabilities' (Koskiaho 1988, 71). Although the pension was low, it does not seem to have affected the living standards of the former workers to any significant degree. Throughout their working life they had lived 'from hand to mouth'. Taking one day at a time in retirement was nothing new. Their deprivation was relative.

Housing provided by Finlayson

When the informants came from the countryside to Tampere and went to work in the mill, they usually moved to one of the flats located in a section of town called Amuri. Finlayson was the owner of these flats in which one kitchen was shared by four households. Two girls usually shared a room. Amuri was originally designed as an area where the factory workers could have built their own little houses. Instead, Finlayson and some private people built rental housing in this area. There were four rooms attached to each kitchen, while each room (about 30 m² in area) housed a separate family or household.

Figure 1   The common kitchen of a Finlayson apartment

The common kitchen was light and quite clean, as the factory periodically inspected its rental houses. There were stairs leading from the kitchen up to storerooms in the garret. In the kitchen, the tenants had one large stove or range for cooking, used by four households, as well as dressers and wash tables with a cover. Under the cover there was a place for a wash pot, basin and a slop bucket. Before running water was installed, each household had its own bucket in the common kitchen. The rooms themselves had stoves for heating, and the tenants sometimes used the stove furnaces for making food. The walls had light wallpaper or boards. The furniture consisted of a table and chairs, a sideboard and one or two folding beds, and a rocking chair.

Usually there were no indoor conveniences, so the water pump and the lavatory were outside. Consequently, everyday chores were difficult to do, especially after a hard day's work. The washing, for example, had to be done on holidays or 'sick days'.

The dwellings with a common kitchen were essential to the factory, but at the same time a cheap form of housing for the workers (Haapala 1986, 65). Because the wages of the informants were quite low, especially in the early years of their working life, getting a room in Amuri, if only a shared one, was considered a luxury. The women could hardly have afforded any other accommodation. Moreover, Amuri was regarded as a good place to live in, since in 1920 there were 2.09 persons per room, less than in housing provided for workers in other industrial towns in the country. In general, in Finland as a whole, there were 2.18 persons per room. 35 per cent of the Finnish population lived in cramped conditions, with more than three persons per room (Jänkälä et al. 1988, 38-40).

Figure 2   Amuri, the suburb of workers

As a section of Tampere, Amuri developed its own distinctive and, in fact, unique character. It was regarded as an almost separate 'little town', a special community of its own. The cobbled streets were characterized by rows of wooden one-storey houses. The privies and other outbuildings dominated the clean yards, which with their birch trees and lilacs offered a beautiful and comforting sight to the onlookers. In the summer the tenants spent a lot of pleasurable time in their yards. In general, people enjoyed their life in Amuri. Although the shared kitchen was cited as a source of frequent arguments, the tenants could always find sociable company and someone to talk to in there. Despite its defects Amuri was a fixed social community with strong neighbourly ties. The general housing conditions and lack of space made it necessary for the tenants to cooperate; at the same time, the conditions also created a framework for social control.

Figure 3   A comfortable yard view in Amuri

When the women got married, they usually moved away from Amuri, first to a rental dwelling with a kitchen and one other room. By the 1920s, this type of housing was the most common among workers. The situation improved in Tampere around 1910 when it was decided that the early traditional type of housing, with the shared kitchen, would no longer be built. New housing areas for workers were constructed and some of the old areas were renovated. The new dwellings had a kitchen and one other room per family, and they also provided conveniences, such as the sink and cold running water. Amuri, however, remained unchanged until the 1960s.

The married women were eventually able to buy a flat of their own. To save money for the flat, the women continued to work. Motherhood usually marked the end of factory work for women, but some of them were forced to continue working just to meet subsistence needs.

In the twenties and thirties, the ideology of the home became popular. Whilst men went out to work, it was emphasized that the woman's place was in the home. Her domestic duties included caring for her children, husband and housework. This, in fact, was a relatively new concept. It represented a more rigid sexual division of labour within the household than had existed in the traditional rural society. It can also be argued that women were to lose a certain degree of their social status because of this. Since housework was not a paid occupation and since it was men who earned the wages, the women's labour and activity were regarded as of less importance (Ahponen & Järvelä 1983, 165). It should be remembered, however, that it was only 'the middle class' women who could live up to this ideal of 'the housewife'. Most other women had to continue to work simply to survive. Indeed, working women were labelled in a negative way in the Finnish society until the ideology of the woman's place in the home finally began to slacken off in the 1950s (Sulkunen 1989, 80-85). Nevertheless, the Finnish women have always participated in the active work force more than the women in the other western countries.

The unmarried women who had remained in Amuri for all their working years were allowed to stay in company lodgings after they retired. The conditions hardly improved during that time, 'cold running water came in and went out'. In the 1960s, Finlayson's began to sell its land property in Amuri as lots for building

54

companies. The women had to move out. The municipality provided housing for the cotton girls in new housing areas far away from the centre. Special provision was made for retired workers. These buildings 'for the elderly' were usually three storeys high and were located next to the other company blocks of flats. Each retired person had one room and a kitchenette, about 25 square metres in area. The flats were equipped with modern conveniences, such as central heating. In an interesting way these flats for retired workers resembled their old work place: a long central passage or corridor with rooms on either side, like the machines in the old factory hall.

Nearly half of the women lived for at least some time in the rental houses for the retired. The women who had lived in the old company flats found the new accommodation 'nice and convenient'. They especially appreciated the comfort and warmth provided by the modern facilities. There was also more privacy since the shared kitchen had been discarded. Their actual living space, however, had decreased and they complained that they were living as if in a box. They missed the old and familiar safety of the Finlayson housing.

Rationally organized final stage of life

As the women grew older and older, they could no longer cope with life in their own homes but had to resort to various, often bureaucratic and inflexible, municipal services. Finally, when they became ill, they had to be hospitalized, and after they could no longer be 'treated' in hospital, they were forced to give up their homes and move to an elderly persons' home, a municipal institution providing residential care for the elderly. Two thirds of the informants in the elderly persons' home had come there directly from hospital. They described their admission to the home, their 'institutionalization', as a traumatic experience, as something truly final and irrevocable. Yet, they did adapt to their new environment, and soon life went on as usual.

The average age of the informants when they moved to the residential home was 78 years. The home is located in a beautiful environment near a lake. The home itself forms a small community with 1,000 residents. In all, there are seven four-storey buildings.

Most of the facilities are shared by several residents, such as the bathroom and the kitchen. Once again the cotton girls were to lose their privacy. In addition to the facilities shared by all, indeed the very structure of the elderly persons' home can be seen as resembling the old factory 'community'. Even the nursing staff can be compared to the old factory staff and its strict hierarchy. However, the old sense of comradeship and belonging no longer prevails in the new environment. The women complained of loneliness and depression. In fact they wished they were dead. The spirit of Finlaysonism was never recaptured.

The retired workers felt that living in an institutionalized setting represented a decline in their life circumstances. Although the women had no financial worries any longer and a sure livelihood was 'provided' for them, they actually preferred their earlier life and their insecure days in the old factory environment. At that time, each day of their life had been a challenge to them: how to meet subsistence needs. This challenge had given 'meaning'[3] and purpose to their life. Despite all the modern comforts of the old people's home, their life was dull.

Conclusions

At the turn of the century women experienced a significant restructuring of their working lives. Agricultural work was replaced by industrial employment. Women were also forced to leave the rural areas — 'home' — and to move to a strange urban setting. They had spent their childhood in a patriarchal household, characterized by 'scanty living', and they felt that the town offered them an opportunity to improve their life circumstances. Childhood experiences had prepared the women well for integration into the patriarchal setting of the factory and the industrial community as a whole. After the absolute poverty of the countryside, the low wages paid by the mill were seen as an improvement, especially for unmarried women. While appreciating the economic factor, the women valued even more the security and the paternal nature of the factory environment. They became the 'subjects' of the mill, and the cheap accommodation kept them tied to the factory. They could not seek other employment since they could not afford to live elsewhere. The factory housing had a significant impact on the women's everyday lives, encouraging them and absorbing them into the spirit of the community — Finlaysonism.

After the demolition of the factory lodgings, the municipality attempted to recapture the old sense of community for the former cotton girls by providing special housing for the elderly. However, the women became isolated from normal social interaction and the local community. This isolation made them feel 'institutionalized', as indeed they were. This feeling culminated in the elderly persons' home. From the days of the shared kitchen and the strong feeling of community and social integration up to the days of the old people's home and its social isolation, the women's housing career changed significantly — and perhaps for the worse — despite the relative improvement in their material conditions. The efforts to integrate the women socially, to recapture 'a sense of community', thus seem to have failed. Later on, when the women were admitted to a geriatric hospital and, consequently, their living space was reduced even further — just a couple of square metres — they regarded this as the final step down on their housing career 'ladder'.

Housing career summary: Physical features and 'community'

— Factory hall

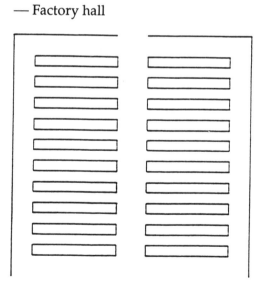

Transmission determined by the rational order of the factory hall with its central passage. Cleanness and control were easy to maintain.

— Lodgings with a shared kitchen

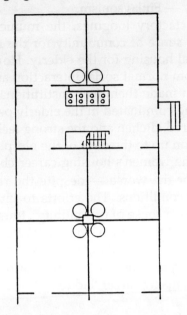

The rationality of the factory hall permeated the order of daily living in factory lodgings. Working and non-working hours controlled by factory ethos. Neighbourly ties were strong and greatly influenced the organization of life.

— Rental lodgings

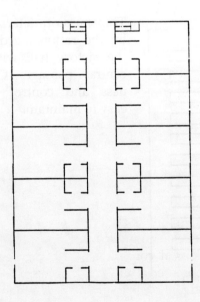

Physically built like the factory halls. Easy to keep clean and maintain. Increased privacy with own kitchenettes and toilets.

— Elderly persons' home

In the last phase of the women's housing career the factory model returned. Privacy was lost once again.

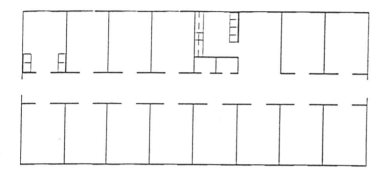

Passages, corridors and close compartments have been the main characteristics of factory housing in Finlayson and, to a certain extent, in other Tampere factory lodgings as well. The 'real' rooms for families employed by factories were the kitchen and 'the chamber' (i.e. the combined bedroom and sitting room).

The old working class people learnt to be realistic as to their chances in life. They never 'reached for the moon'. The goals they set for themselves were attainable, a philosophy inherited from their rural childhood. All through their lives the former Finlayson cotton girls had submitted to authority in one way or another. Throughout their life careers they had moved from one system of control and norms to another. In the old people's home they lost all the norms and meanings that had been of importance to them. Their whole life and all their activities became 'public', as if they were at all times on display for anyone to see.

The elderly informants responded calmly to this final 'stripping' of their physical and psychological conditions, their privacy and individuality. They were depressed, however, because of the absence of social contacts, and they felt their life was lonely and purposeless. They commented that they were satisfied with the care

59

and accommodation provided by the elderly persons' home. A further research project might be in place to explore this topic, but already it seems fair to say that any other kind of residential setting or home would appear strange to these women. Perhaps the women in fact liked the old people's home, because someone there cared about them in the same way as the patron of the factory had done in the old days?

Notes

1. Poor life circumstances were not more pronounced, as Townsend (1979, 50-53) points out, but different generations experience poverty in different ways. This depends on time, conditions, customs and manners.
2. It is also a possible to classify life stages in terms of traditionally defined age stages: childhood 0-11, youth 11-17, adulthood 17 to retirement (Nicholson 1980, 21-22). This is a rigid scheme, however, and does not take into account the differing cultural definitions of particular life stages or the age at which they start.
3. 'Meaning' as a culturally defined framework. In the case of the 'cotton girls' this meaning or framework was brought with them from the countryside — e.g. 'paternal' ideology; the value of hard work and scanty living.

References

Photographs courtesy by Tampere City Archives.

Ahponen, Pirkko-Liisa & Järvelä, Marja (1983), *Maalta kaupunkiin, pientilalta tehtaaseen. Tehdastyöläisten elämäntavan muutos*, WSOY, Helsinki.

Alanen, Antti & Haapala, Pertti (1979), *Työväenluokan synty Tampereella*, Tampereen yliopisto, Sosiologian ja sosiaalipsykologian laitoksen tutkimuksia 37, Tampere.

Alasuutari, Pertti (1986), *Työmiehen elämäntarina ja alkoholismi. Tutkimus alkoholismin suhteesta emokulttuuriin*, Tampereen yliopisto, Sosiologian ja sosiaalipsykologian laitos, sarja A, tutkimuksia 9 (lisensiaattityö), Tampere.

Bertaux, Daniel (ed.) (1981), *Biography and Society. The Life History Approach in the Social Sciences*, SAGE Studies in International Sociology 23, Beverly Hills, California.

Forss, Simo (1982), *Vanhuuseläkkeelle siirtyminen ja hyvinvointi. Tutkimus hyvinvoinnin osatekijöistä ja eläkkeelle valmennuksen merkityksestä vanhuuseläkkeelle siirtymisen yhteydessä*, Eläketurvakeskuksen tutkimuksia 1982:2, Eläketurvakeskus, Mänttä.

Gothoni, Raili (1987), *Pitkäaikaissairaan vanhuksen maailma ja uskonnollisuus*, Suomalaisen teologisen kirjallisuusseuran julkaisuja 149, Helsinki.

Haapala, Pertti (1986), *Tehtaan valossa. Teollistuminen ja työväestön muodostuminen Tampereella 1820-1920*, Suomen historiallinen seura, Historiallisia tutkimuksia 133, Helsinki.

Hemmilä, Pirkko (1981), *Sukupuolten väliset palkkaerot Suomen teollisuudessa vuosina 1936-1978*, Työväen taloudellinen tutkimuslaitos, tutkimuksia, Helsinki.

Jokelainen, Matti (1990), *Eläkeläisten asumistukijärjestelmät kuudessa teollisuusmaassa*, Kansaneläkelaitoksen julkaisuja, M 73, Kansaneläkelaitos, Helsinki.

Jänkälä, Raimo et al. (1988), *Aravavuokratalo 90. Esitutkimus vuokraasuntojärjestelmän kehittämisestä*, Valtion teknillinen tutkimuskeskus, tiedotteita, Espoo 1988.

Koskiaho, Briitta (1988), *Yhteiskunnallistettu vanhuskysymys*, Sosiaalihallituksen julkaisuja 11, Sosiaalihallitus, Helsinki.

Koskiaho, Briitta (1986), *Yhteiskunnan muutos ja sosiaalipolitiikka*, Tammi, Helsinki.

Pättiniemi, Maija-Liisa (1989), *'Pumpulin plikan' elämä. Vanhainkodissa asuvien entisten Finlaysonin naistyöntekijöiden elämäntapa prosessina elämäkertojen perusteella*, Tampereen yliopisto, Sosiaalipolitiikan laitos, pro gradu -tutkielma, Tampere.

Rasila, Viljo (1984), *Tampereen historia, osa 2*, Tampereen kaupunki, Tampereen keskuspaino, Tampere.

Roos, Jeja-Pekka (1988), *Elämäntavasta elämäkertaan. — Elämäntapaa etsimässä 2*, Tutkijaliiton julkaisusarja 53, Tutkijaliitto, Jyväskylä.

Roos, Jeja-Pekka (1987), *Suomalainen elämä. Tutkimus tavallisten suomalaisten elämäkerroista*, Suomalaisen kirjallisuuden seuran toimituksia 454, Suomalaisen kirjallisuuden seura, Helsinki.

Saarenheimo, Marja (1988), *'Elämäkertametodi kokemuksellisuuden tutkimisessa'*, Gerontology, vol. 2, no. 4.

Sulkunen, Irma (1989), *Naisen kutsumus. Miina Sillanpää ja sukupuolten maailmojen erkaantuminen*, Hanki ja jää, Helsinki.

Taimio, Hilkka (1990), *Naisten kotityö ja taloudellinen kasvu Suomessa vuosina 1860-1987, uudelleenarvio*, Elinkeinoelämän tutkimuslaitos, keskustelunaiheita/327, Elinkeinoelämän tutkimuslaitos, Helsinki.

Tolkki-Nikkonen, Mirja (1985), *Kun ei odota ei kärsi, kun ei vaadi ei paljon pety. Yksilön elämänkaaren kriittiset vaiheet*, Tampereen yliopisto, Acta Universitatis Tamperensis Ser A Vol 191, Tampere.

Townsend, Peter (1979), *Poverty in the United Kingdom. A Survey of Household Resources and Standards of Living*, Penguin, Harmondsworth.

4 Elderly people and services – the case of Tampere

Maija-Liisa Pättiniemi

Industrialization, urbanization and the consequent changing of economic and social life started in Finland at the end of last century, much later than in most other western countries. The ageing of the population has also started later. In age structure development, it was not until 60 years later that Finland reached the situation which had prevailed in Sweden as early as 1900. The ageing of the population has, however, been rapid. Finland is today 20 years behind Sweden and will reach Sweden's current age structure in about 2020 (Valkonen and Nikander 1990, 62).

Social changes influence families and their living circumstances. When people have moved from the countryside to town to work in industry, families have decreased in size and living alone has increased. The women have also moved from home to working life and so the provision of care and nursing services in the homes has been reduced. Earlier in the rural society the main responsibility for the care of the elderly traditionally belonged to their families and relatives, and this duty was also stipulated by law; every individual was obliged by law to care for his or her parents and grandparents, and not until 1970 was this obligation finally abolished. When the scope of family responsibility decreased, it was necessary to develop pension and service systems to guarantee the welfare and security of the elderly.

Since the beginning of the 1980s, surveys have been made of the living conditions of the elderly and their use of different support systems in Tampere, the biggest industrial city in Finland. (Haavisto 1984, Heikkinen et al. 1981, Heikkinen J. 1986, Jylhä 1985,

Jyrkämä & Randell 1987, Koskiaho 1986 and 1987, Luokkala 1987, Pättiniemi 1989, Sneck et al. 1987, Vähämäki 1990). Most of these studies have focused on the living conditions of persons aged 75 or over and their need for services, because nowadays the state of health of people aged 65-75[1] and their ability to cope do not markedly differ from the rest of the population. On the basis of these studies, I try to examine the Finnish old age policy and the extent to which it meets the needs of elderly people.

Social security system guarantees a basic livelihood

With the rapid industrialization of Finland, the increasing working class needed social institutions to guarantee material security for itself. At the turn of the century the working class mostly consisted of a population which had its roots in the rural society. People did not earn enough to be able to save money, nor did their earnings cover the expenses caused by illnesses, accidents, unemployment and other social problems. At the time the German view of social security was adopted in Finland. Ensuring economic security did not, however, become legally valid until 1937, when the law on national old age pensions was passed.

After the Second World War the social security system began to expand and became more complicated. The welfare state began to develop. The development of social systems related to work, livelihood and security progressed as the various political parties made decisions about social services. The national old age pension (1937, 1956), the employee pension (in the 1960s), the national health insurance (1963) and the Public Health Act (1972) now guarantee income security for all, including the old and the sick.

The complicated pension system is composed of the national old age pension and the employee pension schemes. All people who live permanently in Finland are covered by these two pension schemes. The total pension of a retired person (60-66 per cent of his or her salary) consists of the employee pension, determined on the basis of the length of the work career and the earned income, and of the national old age pension, which is determined on the basis of the sum total of the employee pension. In other words, the higher the employee pension, the smaller the old age pension.

The basic national old age pension provides basic security in terms of the standard of living for every Finnish person who is 65 years old or unemployed. Since 1984, this scheme has also ensured an early pension for every old citizen (aged 60 to 64) of small means. In general, the legislation concerning elderly people has not taken into consideration women as a special group except for this early pension. According to law, until 1984, the early pension was only paid to women of small means who were 60 to 64 years of age and who lived alone. In addition to the national old age pension, a housing benefit can be paid the sum of which depends on the pensioner's income and housing expenses. The national old age pension is financed jointly by the contributions of insured persons and employees, and of the state and municipalities.

'Everyman's social security' (Sipilä 1979, 64), in the economic sense, was born in the 1960s with the employee pension scheme. The financing depends on the insurance contributions paid by employees, employers and the state. The legal compensation for the national health insurance is financed in the same way. The benefits granted by the national health insurance are important for aged people living at home, because many of them are chronically ill. Among other things, it covers part of the fees of a private doctor, the expenses of examinations and nursing care, and the medicines prescribed by the doctor. The Public Health Act, enforced in 1972, also reduces health care expenses. It obliges the municipalities to maintain health centres providing health counselling and nursing services, including home nursing. In general, health centre services have been free. At the beginning of the 1990s, a very rapid economic recession took the Finnish people by surprise, affecting all public services. The municipalities have decided not to provide free services any longer and have, instead, imposed moderate charges on their services.

The Finnish income security has been considered good internationally. Lately, however, this argument has been criticized and challenged. It is true that the Finnish income security is on a lower level compared with many Central European countries[2], but on the other hand, the benefits are more universal. The system in Finland guarantees basic security against social risks to all persons living in the country and meets their basic needs. In all, it can be said that aged citizens in Finland can live an independent economic life and can also participate fully in society.

In the 1960s it was believed that elderly people's economic

security had been guaranteed by means of the pension systems, so the focus in the care of the elderly shifted to developing a system of services which would best correspond to their needs. The idea was that people using the services would have to say as to what services are provided, and that they could also choose their own services. At the beginning of 1984 a new law on social welfare was enforced, with the aim of maintaining and improving the population's social security and independence. According to the new law, municipalities have to plan the social services for their residents and they may also purchase some services from private providers.[3] This meant that the services of private organizations did not cost the clients any more than the services of the public sector. Buying services is also less expensive for the municipalities than providing their own services.

The City of Tampere tries to perform its legal duties related to social welfare and aims to support elderly people's independent coping at home for as long as possible by providing the aged the kind of holistic care at home as they themselves want and choose. (Social Welfare Office of the City of Tampere 1988.)

Finland-maiden[4] is making the maids of Tampere grey-headed

The proportion of the population aged over 65 grew rather slowly in Finland from the middle of the 19th century to the middle of the 20th century. Since 1950, the proportion of elderly people has increased more rapidly. In 1985 their number was 2.3 times higher than in 1950 (Valkonen and Nikander 1990, 61-64). On the basis of recent mortality rates, about half of women and one fourth of men live up to the age of 80 (Jylhä 1990, 191). Life expectancy has risen rapidly, increasing by about seven years in the last 30 years. In 1989, the life expectancy of women was 79.5 years and that of men 71.5 years.

If we examine the City of Tampere from an international perspective, its short history beginning in 1779 is that of an industrial town, especially a textile industrial town. The concentration of textile industry in Tampere has always been reflected in the greater proportion of women in the population of the town. Because the textile industry employed lots of women, Tampere was a 'women's town' at the beginning of this century. When industry diversified

66

and the relative role of the textile industry decreased, women's greater proportion in the population also began to decrease, although women are still in the majority. In 1990, of the nearly 171,800 residents of Tampere only 53.4 per cent were women, while in 1930 women accounted for 59.0 per cent of the population (The population of Tampere 1990).

Table 1
Women per 1,000 men in Tampere and in Finland

Year	Tampere	Finland
1860	1,336	1,057
1900	1,299	1,026
1940	1,347	1,062
1980	1,166	1,068
1985	1,160	1,065
1990	1,146	1,060

Source: Tampereen väestö 1990 (The population of Tampere 1990), The Office of Statistics, Tampere

In the whole country the figures for women have stayed higher in the last decades. They are now more or less the same compared with the figures of Tampere, where the decrease in the proportion of women has been rapid. Although the excess number of women in Tampere compared with the beginning of the century is at present 11.8 per cent lower, there are still 8.1 per cent more women in Tampere today than in Finland on average.

In some younger age groups in Tampere there are more men, but in the elderly population the excess of women is still significant.

Table 2
The number of male and female persons
by age groups in Tampere in 1990

Age	Men	Women	The number of women as a percentage of the number of men
0 - 4	4,842	4,696	-3.0
10-14	4,739	4,561	-3.8
20-24	6,209	6,681	7.6
30-34	7,091	6,774	-4.8
40-44	7,747	7,892	1.9
50-54	4,616	5,225	13.2
60-64	3,804	5,148	35.3
70-74	1,974	4,069	106.1
80-84	862	2,532	193.7
90-94	78	337	332.1
95 -	8	49	512.5

Source: Tampereen väestö 1990 (The population of Tampere 1990),
The Office of Statistics, Tampere.

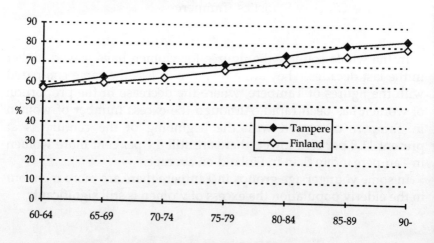

Figure 1 Women's proportion in each age group of 5 years in Tampere and in Finland in 1985

Source: Tampereen väestö 1990 (The population of Tampere 1990),
The Office of Statistics, Tampere.

In 1990, there were 24,700 retired people over 65 years of age living in Tampere. They accounted for 14.4 per cent of the whole population, which is a little more than the corresponding figure for the whole country (13.9). A total of 10,660 people (6.2 per cent of the population), 2,840 men and 7,820 women, were over 75 years old. Of the men, 62.8 per cent were married, compared with only 14.5 per cent of women. The 'women's town' has changed into a 'town of old women living alone'.

The Finnish legislation contains no laws which would take aged women as a special group into consideration, but because of the clearly greater number of women it can be said that when we talk about elderly people and their needs, we talk especially about aged women and their needs.

The over 75-year-old Finnish people belong to the generation of wars and shortage (Roos 1987, 53). First of all, there was the Civil War, associated with Finland's independence in 1917-18, and secondly, the Second World War in 1939-45. Periods of shortage followed both of these wars; the country had also suffered from the depression of the early 1930s which had affected the whole world. The central focus in life for women, work or family, has depended on whether they have been married or single. In old age, however, lifestyles become more similar and cross the boundaries of social classes (Gothoni 1990, 19). Yet elderly people are not a homogeneous group in their ways of life; their views of life and their values vary. The basic influences on lifestyle are formed during early years and lead to the survival of social group differences in the years after retirement (Jylhä 1990, 185). Nevertheless, some common features can be pointed out. For example, the aged women of today are satisfied with little, because they have lived through the wartime and days of shortage and have been compelled to struggle for their daily bread. The present social and economic security means progress to them and some of them may even find it difficult to adapt to it.

For an old woman, being a woman means being 'submissive and unassuming and minding her own way of life. The woman is self-sacrificing, responsible, tenacious and hard working. The woman is a real carer, who assumes responsibility for the welfare of her children and the other family members'. This is why the woman should be proud of her femininity. Ultimately it is the woman who is the maintainer of society and the provider of life. (Ronkainen

1990, 115.) The life structure of the female generation who have experienced the wartime and shortage has been simple. The central factor of their life has been the unit consisting of the home and the family. The women have learnt to live traditionally in passive roles, submissive to men. They have become passively dependent family members. This is true of aged Finnish women, although the Finnish women's practical and legal status as a whole has for decades been better than the women's status in Central Europe, for example. Women have always worked outside the home; in particular, they have worked full time. Working full time has always been more general in Finland than in the other Nordic Countries, where women's part-time employment has been quite common.

The development of Finland into a welfare state has to a large extent depended on women's work. When social services began to develop in the 1970s, women's working increased further, especially in the public sector and service employment. In 1987, women already accounted for 50 per cent of the labour force (Lilja et al. 1990, 762). This high number of women working outside the home is one reason why in the present urban nuclear family there is no space for the aged parents. It is true that old people prefer to live independently in their own dwellings. They have the opportunity to retain their independence in contrast to their parents who, when old, lived in three-generation families in the countryside. In the welfare state, however, the independence of elderly people is very limited. When the ability to cope decreases, the dependence on other people increases. Today dependence on the authorities has taken the place of dependence on relatives. The model of caring has changed. Most women of the war and shortage generation have a rural background, and it was clearly their responsibility to care for their parents as well as possible. Even the law obliged them to care for their parents, but they also cared for other relatives.

Health is a central concern of elderly people. Since women live longer, they are more likely to develop a chronic illness or disability which limits their physical mobility. The diseases of the circulatory system[5] constitute the biggest group: coronary diseases, insufficiency of the heart, blood pressure, and disorders of the cerebral circulation which are the most probable causes of strokes. Cancer and the diseases of the joints and the back are also common. The locomotor diseases seldom result in death, but at present they are the most rapidly increasing group of diseases. Some 27 per cent of over 75-year-old men and 36 per cent of women suffer from these diseases. Dementia is also increasing. About one tenth of persons aged 75 to 84, and 17 per cent of those aged 85 or over suffer from moderate or serious dementia (Jylhä 1990, 171-172).

Social class has been shown to shape the dimensions of health, and old people belonging to lower occupational groups have more illnesses than those belonging to higher occupational groups. They are also less able to cope (Jylhä 1990, 184).

In terms of self-perceived health, aged women consider themselves chronically ill more frequently than men (women 22 per cent, men 17 per cent). Because of their illnesses and poor coping skills elderly people frequently seek various health services. A typical client of the health centre is an aged woman who lives alone (Sauli et al. 1989, 82).

Undervalued and underpaid work by women is reflected in the standard of living in old age

In 1989, one third of pensioners received only the national old age pension, and of them 98 per cent were over 65 years old. Women made up 75 per cent of them. If the old age pension is a woman's only income, she usually belongs to the older age group. The national old age pension is the sole income for 22 per cent of women aged 65-79 and for 43 per cent of those over 80. (The corresponding percentages for men are 8 and 24.) These women have generally been housewives in towns or in the countryside. A widow is paid a certain part of the spouse's pension as a widow's pension, but divorced women do not get this benefit. The proportion of divorces among old people has increased in the 1980s. Divorces in towns are more common than in the countryside, which is attributable to cultural differences and the stricter social control in the rural areas (Gothoni 1990). In agriculture, marriage is still based on work companionship and in general the union is not broken, even if matrimonial happiness should fade.

With regard to education, 84 per cent of the women aged 65 or over have only gone to elementary school (78 per cent of men), while four per cent have a college level education (9 per cent of men) (Sauli 1989, 58). In their childhood, many of the people aged

75 or over suffered from insecurity and deprivation, and many could not finish school. With no schooling and unskilled as workers they have had no choice in the labour market. Older women worked in low paid service and industrial occupations, in Tampere mostly in textile industry. Even today the wages are the lowest in those jobs in which the labour force is predominantly female. This traditional worldwide model is also repeated in Finland despite the high rate of unionization among both male and female workers. Even today Finnish women still earn 25 per cent less on average than men (Lilja et al. 1990, 158-165). Since the employee pension is bound to earnings, the total pensions of aged women are over 28 per cent lower on average than those of men.

On the basis of statistics, older women are economically the worst off, but in fact they experience their economic situation as satisfactory (Gothoni 1990, 47). Their satisfaction reflects the fact that these aged women experienced the wartime and the postwar shortage and have thus become accustomed to living on little money. They consider their income in every respect satisfactory and lead an economically independent life. Not until their ability to cope begins to weaken does the question of getting help from society and/or family arise.

The types of housing for elderly people

The basic elements of elderly people's welfare consist of housing and support services. Housing and the physical environment have a great impact on the extent to which the elderly are able to cope after their physical condition begins to deteriorate. Meeting elderly people's housing needs is very important because old people with limited mobility live a very house-centred life. Their housing has to meet many needs.

On the basis of old people's housing needs and their need for care, including nursing care, a number of steps or phases can be distinguished in the system of old age care. When people grow old, their illnesses increase and their ability to cope weakens. Even with support, coping at home may prove impossible; then moving to a place where care services can be provided more efficiently becomes necessary. In Tampere the stages in elderly people's housing range from independent living at home through supported housing and a residential home or elderly persons' home finally to a geriatric hospital.

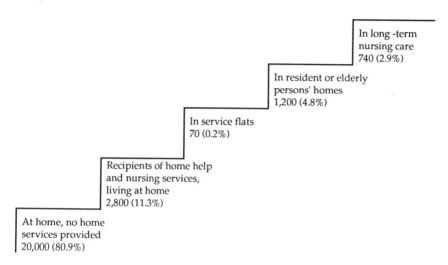

In long -term
nursing care
740 (2.9%)

In resident or elderly
persons' homes
1,200 (4.8%)

In service flats
70 (0.2%)

Recipients of home help
and nursing services,
living at home
2,800 (11.3%)

At home, no home
services provided
20,000 (80.9%)

Figure 2 The housing of people aged 65 and over in Tampere in 1991

The largest part of the pensioners in Tampere, 92 per cent, live at home. This figure includes aged persons living in their own or rented flats, as well as those living in special service flats or rental housing for the retired. Some 75 per cent of those aged 75 or over live in their own dwellings, 20 per cent of them in small houses. According to the 1985 census, elderly people have more space than the rest of the population, and they seldom suffer from a real shortage of housing. In 1987, for example, about 1,000 persons queued for dwellings let by the municipality. Only 10 per cent of them were over 65 years old. However, the standard equipment of their housing is on average below that of all residents' in the city. About 20 per cent of elderly people in Tampere live with inadequate facilities, which is less than in the rest of Finland (30 per cent), however. In most cases they lack conveniences such as bathroom or shower room, warm water, and central or electric heating. (The Housing Programme of the City of Tampere 1990-1994.)

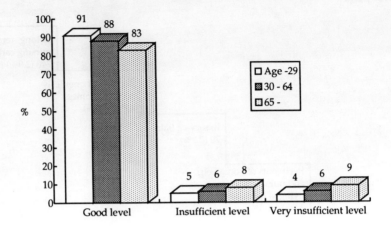

Figure 3 The age and housing of the population in Tampere according to the 1985 census

Source: The Housing Programme of the City of Tampere, 1990-1994

Converting the existing flats of elderly people to the needs of the residents constitutes a real problem in Tampere. Living in insufficiently equipped housing increases the need for services. In the whole of the country unsatisfactory housing leads to the need of the elderly for institutional care. According to the 1987 survey (Luokkala 1987), Tampere residents aged 75 and over mostly hoped for practical improvements in their flats, such as fitting a shower or renovating the bathroom, removing thresholds and making some other small changes. In other words, without these repairs, their day-to-day coping was difficult. The necessity of improving the housing of the elderly has been recognized by authorities, but the funds for carrying out the repair work have been inadequate. In general, elderly people themselves only want basic improvements. This is not because of shortage of money; old people are simply afraid of all the trouble caused by the repair work and frequently find it difficult to adapt to changes.

74

The housing continuum

Home services

The housing situation of elderly people in Tampere is reasonably good. Coping with daily tasks and activities is increasingly a problem related to housing. Coping at home is supported by various home services and home nursing. Home services are provided on the basis of disability, stress, illness, injury or some similar reason.

The national plans related to the organization of social welfare and health care (National Board of Social Welfare 2/1988) emphasize domestic care and the integration of social and health services. According to national instructions, municipalities have to develop service networks to support old people living at home. Besides round-the-clock domestic care, this means changing institutional care so that it can be used flexibly: care can be provided for a short time, for part of the day or for a weekend. Local authorities, parishes, organizations and voluntary associations cooperate in developing the various services. Home service is a social service meant for all those who need it, irrespective of their financial status.

The delivery of municipal home services is controlled by the board of social welfare. These services include meals on wheels, hygiene, cleaning, clothes care, transportation and escort services, for example. On the other hand, home nursing services are controlled by the board of health care, and they include services such as consulting a doctor, nurse or physiotherapist, health care services in general, provision of assistive devices, and rehabilitation.

As mentioned above, in Tampere the population structure of the clients aged 75 or over who receive home services is quite special. Over 81 per cent of them are women, 80 per cent of them live alone and six per cent of them have no contacts even to their relatives. Of the over 85-year-olds living alone, former female industrial women workers who are single and live alone receive the biggest proportion of home services in Tampere (30 per cent). Of the recipients of home services over 14 per cent live with their spouses. Of those who live at home without any domestic services, over 36 per cent are married. It is more rare for couples to receive home services, because generally one or the other of them, usually the wife, takes care of the daily housework. This reflects the traditional division of labour (Luokkala 1987).

According to the survey made in 1987 (Luokkala 1987), 84 per cent of people over 75 years old in Tampere use no services. Almost 78 per cent of men belong to this group, so men receiving services are in the minority. One third of aged persons who receive no services (and 15 per cent of recipients) have worked as higher executives or officials. They generally live in their own flats of two or three rooms and a kitchen (70 per cent), or in small houses or flats with their spouses or relatives (50 per cent). Their life is not lonely and they are in good health. In general, they do not want to leave their homes, not even to move to a service flat (80 per cent), but would rather like services to be brought to their home (30 per cent). Only 3.5 per cent of the persons who receive no services are willing to move to a residential home or an elderly persons' home (Luokkala 1987).

The health of all recipients of home services has deteriorated to some extent. According to their own assessment they are in poor health (56 per cent), and eight per cent of the clients suffer from dementia. Poor health means disability and declining mobility. Two thirds of home service clients are in such poor health that they find it difficult to participate in activities outside their home. One third of home service clients live in small flats — one room and a kitchenette — in rental housing built for aged people of small means. They more often feel lonely and insecure (47.5 per cent) than people living independently (21.5 per cent). Although satisfied with their flats, many would be quite willing to move to the elderly persons' home (12.6 per cent).

Most home service recipients need help in cooking and cleaning, but they also need help in washing, shopping and running errands. Relatives play an important role in supporting their elderly. In fact, people often prefer help given by their own relatives and only resort to the help provided by the municipality as a secondary source of support. Research shows that 89 per cent of the clients are satisfied with the help they receive. Nevertheless these elderly persons would actually need more help (64 per cent). Their dissatisfaction, especially with the help in cleaning, has come out in public discussion. Extensive or non-routine house cleaning is not part of the work of municipal home service workers. They only do normal daily cleaning. The demand for help in more extensive cleaning was rejected by the municipality in 1989 on the grounds that extending municipal cleaning help to the over 65-year-olds would have meant an increase in taxes. The fact is, however, that only a small minority of people aged 65 and over actually need help in cleaning. After the municipality had rejected the request, voluntary organizations began to provide this service, but their contribution does not meet the need. Old people must turn to their relatives or private firms for help.

Living alone and declining health are factors which clearly increase the need for services. Preventive action, which would support elderly people's independent living at home, has not yet been realized in Tampere. Provision of services is insufficient, because the resources for domestic care are too small. Services have not been able to offer help to all those needing it. According to the survey by Luokkala (Luokkala 1987), the municipal home services are appropriately targeted. The home service clients are aged, and in terms of health and economic status they are worse off compared with the old persons not receiving these services.

Service centre as a support for independent living

The above survey (Luokkala 1987) showed clearly that elderly people want to live in their own homes for as long as possible, but they would like to have a service centre for the elderly near their home. However, they do not actually use the services of the centre except for meals[6]. The same result was obtained in a similar study (Vähämäki 1990) which examined the welfare of people who were 75 years old or over and who lived in the vicinity of either a private or a municipal service centre for the elderly.

The private service centre which was studied is located in the centre of Tampere. Of the aged people living near the centre, 67 per cent are women. About 20 per cent of them are single, 65 per cent are widows and 12 per cent married. Of the men, 67 per cent are married. These elderly people belong to the same group as those elderly who live at home and receive no services (70 per cent) (Vähämäki 1990). The men of this group seem to live in a situation in which they receive the needed help from their spouses. These elderly people living in the vicinity of the private service centre are satisfied with their life and feel it has continued unchanged after they moved near the service centre. An obvious explanation is that nearly all of these people used to live in a block of flats in the centre of the city. About one half of them used to live in their own flats. All are satisfied with their present housing and their economic situation is good. Most of them belong to the middle or upper class (74 per cent). They have maintained their social relationships and have no feeling of insecurity. Concern about safety is further relieved by an alarm system which enables them to get help round the clock; contacting the service centre happens automatically by phone. The study shows that old people really appreciate this service which guarantees them full security. In fact, they regard it as more important than any other services that they are provided.

The flats situated in connection with the municipal service centre for the elderly, or in its vicinity, were originally intended for pensioners of small means living in substandard housing in Tampere. Women, 38 per cent of them single, make up 83 per cent of the residents. They have mostly worked in industrial or service occupations (80 per cent) and therefore their economic status is worse than that of the people living in the vicinity of the private service centre. The residents of the municipal service centre used to live in small houses in a suburb (54 per cent), in a more or less rural environment. Only 17 per cent of them owned their former dwellings. Most of them are satisfied with their present housing (63 per cent), although the washing rooms are not regarded as adequate. Some 11 per cent of the residents have openly expressed their dissatisfaction. The overall satisfaction of the residents with their housing may be due to the beautiful site of the building close to nature in the outskirts of the city. Also, people have been able to stay in a familiar environment, which is comforting to them. Of the residents, 18 per cent receive municipal home services, which would seem too little for the need, since 46 per cent of them also receive help from their relatives and friends.

The experiences of loneliness, insecurity and illness are apparently common among the residents of the municipal service centre. Only a small proportion of the residents who were studied felt their life was safe and secure. These aged persons frequently feel unsafe in contrast to old people living at home and receiving domestic help. The lack of an alarm system in the flats of the service centre contributes in a major way to the feelings of insecurity and fear which are at their height at weekends and nights, when there are no staff on duty in the service centre.

The residents who have moved to the flats near the private service centre or in connection with the municipal service centre have deliberately chosen their current type of housing. In the rental housing situated near or in connection with the municipal service centre, the residents are mostly women who belong to the working class. They have low incomes and their health status is poor. Only a few of them feel secure. Almost all of them would like to have services that would reduce their anxiety, and 27 per cent would like to receive more services. In the vicinity of the private service centre, on the other hand, the residents are women and couples who belong to the middle and upper classes. Their incomes are higher and their health status is good. They buy over 50 per cent of their services from private providers. Some five per cent of them would like to receive more services. They experience their housing as safe. Their flats really fulfil the criteria of service housing defined by the Tampere board of social welfare. These criteria comply with the instructions of the National Board of Social Welfare:

— the residents' independent housing is monitored and supported daily;

— the residents in independent housing are provided with at least a meal service and the necessary hygiene, as well as cleaning, shopping and professional services;

— the flats must have a safety alarm system which enables the residents to get help round the clock; and

— service housing does not necessarily presume a round-the-clock staff, but a 24-hour emergency duty is required. (The Social Welfare Office of the City of Tampere 1988, 15-16.)

The safety alarm system makes the biggest difference between housing in an ordinary flat and in a service flat.

In 1990, two new buildings for elderly people were completed in Tampere, a new municipal building and another private one. A safety alarm system was installed in the private building, but not in the municipal one because of the high cost of the system. According to the instructions of the National Board of Social Welfare, Tampere should have had about 350 service flats by the end of 1991. Without the contribution of private organizations this objective could not have been reached.

The development of different forms of service in Tampere has entailed establishment of community clubs in support of home services. The municipal community clubs have tried to create some kind of a network for old age care. The clubs offer meals, hobbies and recreational activities for pensioners in the immediate neighbourhood. In the different areas of the city there are at present five clubs. In addition, there are two municipal day hospitals and a day care centre for the elderly. Among other things, they offer meals, health care, hygiene and recreation services.

Care in residential homes for elderly persons

The waiting lists for elderly persons' homes and residential homes are long, and applications are numerous. The need for institutional care should not be calculated by the number of applications, however. Aged persons apply for residential home places 'just to make sure' because of the lack of home services and service flats. Since alternative forms of housing are insufficient, institutional care is an inevitable solution in Tampere for an aged person whose initiative and coping skills have impaired significantly and permanently.

Tampere has one municipal elderly persons' home with nearly 1,000 care places located in seven blocks of flats. Two of the 32 departments of this home, about 9 per cent, have been converted into wards for chronically ill patients. In the private residential homes there are about 250 care places. About 80 per cent of the residents of these homes are women.

From the viewpoint of society, residential home care in Finland is 'economically the most profitable' form of care, because the fee is determined as 80 per cent of the elderly person's net income. This may be one reason why authorities so readily institutionalize elderly people. In comparison with the other Nordic Countries there are more institutional places in Finland in relation to the number of elderly people. In Tampere the number of institutional places does not exceed the National Board of Social Welfare recommendation which is 18 per cent of the over 75-year-old people in the municipality. The National Board of Social Welfare intends to reduce the number of institutional places to 10-12 per cent of the 75-year-olds by the year 2000.

According to the instructions of the National Board of Social

Welfare, ten per cent of residential home places must be short-term care places. This goal has been reached in Tampere. Some 120 short-term places have been provided for aged persons who need home care support, general care and social rehabilitation in a residential home. Short-term care, which may last from one to four weeks, is quite popular and the demand for places is great. Occasionally places have been reserved six months in advance. There should be far more short-term places, however. Despite help from relatives, carers of the aged need relief, and this kind of care is even economically profitable. For example, in the geriatric hospital in Tampere in July 1991 there were 20 aged persons who could not be sent home. They no longer needed hospital care, but they could only have been discharged after an observation and rehabilitation period. Because of the lack of short-term places, they had to stay on in hospital, where the costs for care are two and a half times higher than in a residential home.

It has been estimated that every third residential place and every fifth long-term care place in the health centre have been poorly assigned. However, the staff of the residential homes in Tampere have estimated that 84 per cent of the residents are in the 'right' place. In its assessment of care needs of elderly people in Tampere, a review group in turn commented that in 1988 at least one half or even more of the elderly persons in the residential homes of Tampere could have managed at home, if home services had been sufficient and if more short-term care and different day care services had been provided. Similarly, more flats should be repaired and converted. (The Social Welfare Office of the City of Tampere 1988, 32.) The only real alternatives to residential housing, service housing and other support are provided by private organizations whose resources, however, are quite small. Consequently, they are unable to offer real alternative solutions to the problems of the housing of the elderly.

The only municipal elderly persons' home in Tampere is an enormous organization with 1,000 places and large administration. There are about 600 employees in this institution of whom some 350 belong to the nursing staff. The large administration is reflected in the costs: in 1991 the net cost per care day was 30 per cent higher than the net cost per day in one of the largest private residential homes with 62 places.

The average age of residents is mostly equally high, about 84 years, both in the municipal elderly persons' home and the private residential homes. In some private homes the average age may even be one year higher than in the municipal home. Therefore, the poorer health status of the residents of the municipal home is not dependent on the age of the residents. The decisive factor seems to be the social background of the residents. The aged from the upper social classes get selected to the private residential homes, while the residents of the municipal home mostly belong to the working class. The average care fees paid by the residents clearly indicate this difference. In the private homes the residents pay 40 per cent higher care fees per month on average than the residents of the municipal home. The residents' poorer health status in the municipal home may be a consequence of their severe living conditions and hard working life.

Elderly people as an object group of social policy in Tampere

In the City of Tampere, the social and health care services which aim to support elderly people's coping are largely directed to the section of the elderly population who are the worst off in terms of independence and economy. The municipality buys nearly all services provided by private organizations and thus the costs are the same for the users of both private and municipal services. The users of private or municipal services are clearly selected on social grounds, however. The users of municipal services are mainly people living alone, mostly working class women of small means and in worse health. The users of private services belong to the middle or upper classes and are economically well-to-do widows and couples in fairly good health.

The reason for this social selection to 'class A or class B of aged citizens' may be explained by the history of industrial Tampere. Attitudes are a major barrier, while issues related to administration or resources are less significant. When I have interviewed aged people both in the private and municipal homes this has come out clearly: the few factory workers, cleaners and shop assistants living in the private homes do not feel that they belong. Their social class is different from the majority of the residents. They experience the home as a different world and because of that they do not feel happy there. In general, when class conscious aged persons who have worked in industrial or service occupations are forced to choose between private and municipal services, they prefer the latter. On the basis of their life histories they make a distinction between 'municipal' and 'private'. To them 'private' means expensive and something that does not meet their needs.

Municipal interventions in old age care in Tampere do not meet the people's needs. As regards the problem of housing for the elderly, much anxiety and insecurity arises from living alone and in poor health. The feeling of security means that when in need one can contact a source of help or a support person at any time. When the request for help is responded to, it is clearly reflected in how satisfied people are with their own situation. An adequate knowledge of available services naturally has an effect on how one seeks help. It is more than obvious that there is a need for local service centres for elderly people, for a safety alarm system, for weekend and evening services, and for short-term care places in Tampere.

The proportion of women in the labour force has always been high in Finland. Consequently, it is part of the Finnish culture that elderly persons emphasize the duty of society to provide enough social and health care services. Elderly people want to live independently and do not want to be a burden to their relatives.

During the recent economic recession, attempts have been made to restrain social expenditure. As the income of the public sector decreases, the welfare state must reduce its consumption. The state has directed its subsidies to certain services purchased by the municipalities. This trend came to an end in 1993, when the system of state funding was changed. Now the state subsidy is given to the municipalities as a lump sum which the municipalities can then divide between the different social sectors as they wish. Municipal grants to private service providers may be cut by reducing the number of service contracts made by the municipality. As a result, private services will be much more expensive. This in turn will mean even a more distinct division of elderly people into class A and class B citizens. On the basis of economic resources, elderly people will be classified into the 'self paying' users of private services and the 'poor of the municipality'. If social and health care expenditure is cut considerably, people will not only be classified into the poor and the rich but, in addition, illness and health will be used as the criteria for classification. Then the chronically ill, even if wealthy, may have to spend all their income on being treated and cared for. When an aged person is no longer able to buy health services, he or she will be faced with institutional care provided by the municipality.

Elderly people's life situations are dependent on the values of society and its political and economic decision-making. In Finland, as well as in the other Nordic Countries, the care of the elderly is of a high standard from an international perspective. The Finnish welfare state has been able to provide services at a moderate cost and income security has also been good by international standards. In comparison with Denmark and Sweden, the care of the elderly in Finland puts more emphasis on institutional care. The problem in old age care is the quality and one-sidedness of the services and the lack of humanity. Alternative forms of housing combined with specific services are only at an experimental and developmental stage. We have reason to believe that both the quantity and the quality of the services of the welfare state will decrease because of lack of money. It is above all the elderly people who will suffer from the cuts of the welfare state, because more than one half of all social expenditure is directed to them. When the public services no longer suffice, new strategies must be found to guarantee an acceptable level of social security.

Finland is facing a difficult situation: its population is ageing rapidly and the country is suffering from the consequences of a serious economic recession. Will the country now resort to the strategy of using women as underpaid care employees or even as unpaid voluntary carers to respond to the increasing service needs of social and health care?

Voluntary work

Grannie's Room and Koukkuniemi Elderly Persons' Home

The Finnish social policy legislation contains a number of stipulations which oblige social welfare authorities to cooperate with other municipal authorities and organizations whose activities are closely related to the tasks of social welfare (Virta-Toivola 1993, 21). Professional social workers have traditionally objected to the use of voluntary workers in tasks related to social work. Voluntary

84

work by lay persons continues, however, even though this activity became rather marginal at one point as the official system of social work expanded.

As the resources of the public sector have been cut down since the early 1990s, efforts have been made to compensate for this reduction by means of self-care, family carers, neighbourly help and other community work. In practice, a new kind of division of labour has been established between experts providing professional help and lay volunteers providing community help. There is not much room for community help in traditional institutional care, but today community work is finding its place even in institutions.

Education and professionalism are the traditional hallmarks of the work community in the care of the elderly. The hierarchically organized group of workers have specific job descriptions, partly defined by their education, as well as by legislation and trade union agreements. In the last few years, new models of thinking have brought a new kind of humanity into the institutional care of the elderly. The old hierarchical structures are being pulled down and the elderly persons are treated holistically as individuals, not just as objects of care. After society was faced with the recent economic crisis, costs of labour have had to be cut by reducing staff, for example. This has resulted in a lot of frustration among employees. Their possibilities of carrying out their work in accordance with the new ideology and new methods have been far too limited compared with the resources available to them.

Voluntary work in the present dire economic situation may help maintain those services for which the resources of the professional staff are not sufficient. In return, the professionals can concentrate on delivering the actual care to their patients or clients.

In 1988, a group of people in Tampere met to discuss voluntary work and its possibilities. They decided to launch an experiment using voluntary workers in a new way that had not been experimented with before. This marked the beginning of a project called Grannie's Room. The group found premises for Grannie's Room, an office, a couple of rooms and a kitchen. The project was ready to start its "open house" for elderly persons. It was quite soon discovered that there is a lot of distress in society; many people need help, not only the elderly but also families and the handicapped. Today this voluntary work centre is rapidly growing from its modest one employee and one base beginning, and similar

Grannie's Rooms are now being established all over the country. There is one even in Spain for retired Finnish people living there. In Tampere the premises as well as the activities have expanded continuously, and two more office employees have been hired to organize the work of the volunteers.

Voluntary work is unpaid work. Only the travel costs of the workers are reimbursed. In the first few years the number of voluntary workers kept growing steadily. In 1992, they amounted to 300 persons and in 1993 to as many as 1,200. So far, it has been possible to respond to all requests for help, and volunteers have also been precepted to work as support persons for people living in institutions in Tampere.

The elderly persons' home of Koukkuniemi in Tampere is situated in a peaceful environment on Lake Näsijärvi some two kilometres away from the centre of town. The home consists of seven four-storey buildings. These blocks of flats are divided into departments each of which has 30 residents and about ten employees. Since institutional care is the ultimate form of care for the elderly, the functional abilities of the residents are already deteriorated as a result of various disorders. The resources of the staff are tied up in providing just basic nursing care; consequently, they only have a limited amount of time available for interaction with the residents or helping them individually. This has created a real challenge for voluntary workers in the elderly persons' home.

The church, the Red Cross and the war veteran organizations have done voluntary work in Koukkuniemi since the 1970s, mainly in the form friendship service. This activity has been rather limited, however, and has not been very visible. Friendship service has generally begun as personal help at home, and it just continues after the resident has moved to the elderly persons' home. Voluntary "friends" have never talked much about their work in public, partly because their work in the elderly persons' home has not been valued.

The voluntary work in connection with the Grannie's Room is organized differently from that of other associations. Grannie's Room looks for voluntary workers to respond specifically to the needs of the residents in the elderly persons' home. The number of workers has risen in Koukkuniemi, too, as the activities of Grannie's Room have expanded. In the first couple of years, only a few retired people did voluntary work in Koukkuniemi, but in 1993 their number increased significantly, amounting to about 60 in all. Many of the new volunteers were unemployed, among them young unemployed persons.

In addition to voluntary workers who themselves offer their services to Grannie's Room, volunteers are also sought by means of advertisements in local papers. There are various orientation courses for new workers who are also given a package of information. Afterwards, they can then decide for themselves, whether voluntary work in the elderly persons' home is something they would like to do. If they decide to continue, they will register through Grannie's Room. All voluntary work in Koukkuniemi is contracted through Grannie's Room.

In principle, the work of voluntary employees is quite independent and flexible. There are no strict contracts or agreements. The volunteers come to the elderly persons' home specifically to help the residents in all kinds of small tasks. For example, they may escort the residents to the bank, go shopping with them, take them to special events organized in the home, go to the theatre with them, or on an excursion, etc. Some voluntary workers have eventually ended up as some kind of assistants to the professional staff. For example, they may do "housework" in the departments, take care of the linen or mend the residents' clothes, etc.

The café of the elderly persons' home used to be closed at weekends because of shortage of staff. The residents wanted the café to be kept open at weekends, too, so that they could go and have a cup of coffee there with their relatives and friends. Grannie's Room helped find a number of voluntary workers and with their help café services are now provided every day of the week.

Conclusions concerning voluntary work

The attitudes of the staff of the elderly persons' home towards voluntary workers has changed over time. At first the members of staff were quite indifferent or at times professionally patronizing. Gradually, however, they learnt to accept and appreciate voluntary work, and how to benefit from the knowledge and skills of the volunteers. This change of attitude is reflected in the greater "demand" for voluntary workers.

The contribution of the voluntary workers of Grannie's Room is in many ways visible in the life of Koukkuniemi elderly persons' home. Residents now participate more actively in the various events organized in the home, and the café with its services is open for residents and their visitors even at weekends. Voluntary work brings new richness to the life of the home, improving the community spirit.

Voluntary work at its best means human interaction: the worker not only gives, but also receives. Nearly 90 per cent of those who are committed to voluntary work have stayed with the project, which certainly indicates that they really gain something valuable from their experience and that this work is meaningful to them.

As the number of voluntary workers has increased, they have felt the need to exchange ideas and experiences with other volunteers. After all, working in a huge organization a volunteer may sometimes feel quite alone; he or she seldom comes across another voluntary worker in the work community. There are plans now to establish a Grannie's Room of its own in Koukkuniemi, so that the volunteers working in the home would have a place where they could meet each other, have a rest, arrange small events, etc. The future role of this new Grannie's Room will depend on the ideas and aspirations of the volunteers themselves but also on the ability of the elderly persons' home to respond to the challenges of voluntary work. Cooperation between the professional staff and the voluntary workers is clearly beginning to find its proper format. It is fair to conclude that voluntary work is now establishing its place and position in municipal institutional care in Tampere.

Notes

1. In Finland the ordinary retirement age is 65 years. In the public sector, however, the age is 63 years.
2. The comparison of social security and basic living standards in different countries is very difficult. European states have been divided as to organization of welfare. According to the model of the Nordic countries, the citizens' livelihood must be secured irrespective of market fluctuations. Central European countries, in contrast, establish their social policy on interest organizations and the central position of employment (Arajärvi and Skinnari 1990, 242). The purchasing power of elderly people whose

pensions are bound to the earnings of their work career is influenced by the various wage and price levels of the different countries. One proof of the good standard of living of the Nordic countries is that there are few pensioners among the recipients of basic social benefits. According to poverty studies based on incomes, the poverty risk is low (Uusitalo, 1991). Of the Nordic countries at least in Sweden and Denmark, elderly people enjoy a better livelihood than the elderly in Finland. These countries are also wealthier than Finland.

3. The municipalities make contracts with private organizations to buy services provided by them. In the contract, the care and service fees are determined on an equal basis for all clients, be they clients of the public or the private sector. The municipality compensates the private organizations for the losses caused by this work, while the state subsidizes the municipalities for 40 per cent of their loss.

4. The phrase 'Finland-maiden' derives from the geographical form of Finland. If you look at Finland on the map the form of the country resembles a female body.

5. In a national interview study on health made in the 1970s, about two thirds of the Finnish women aged 54 or over and half of the men mentioned that they suffered from some disease of the circulatory system (Klaukka 1982, 59).

6. The services of the centre for the elderly include, for example, a restaurant, meals on wheels, health care, nursing care, various hobbies, and other recreation and leisure activities.

References

Arajärvi, Pentti ja Skinnari, Jouko (1990), *Eurooppa ja Suomi. Euroopan taloudellinen yhdentyminen, työelämä ja sosiaaliturva*, Sosiaaliturvan Keskusliitto, Helsinki.

Bourdier, Pierre (1985), *Sosiologian kysymyksiä*, Vastapaino, Tampere (Gummerus).

Gothoni, Raili (1990), *Vanhusten sosiaaliset verkostot ja sosiaalinen tuki*, Tutkimus kalliolaisten ja kiteeläisten vanhusten elämäntilanteesta, sosiaalisista verkostoista ja tuesta, Sosiaali- ja terveysministeriö, suunnitteluosaston julkaisuja 2/1990, Helsinki.

Haavisto, Matti (1984), *85 vuotta täyttäneiden tamperelaisten elinolot ja terveydentila*, Tampereen yliopisto, Acta Universitatis Tamperensis Ser A Vol 175 (Lääketieteellisen tiedekunnan julkaisuja 58), Tampere.

Heikkinen, Eino et al. (1981), *Eläkeikäiset Tampereella*, Haastattelututkimus 60-89-vuotiaiden tamperelaisten terveydentilasta, toimintakykyisyydestä, palvelujen käytöstä ja elintavoista, Tampereen yliopisto, Kansanterveystieteen julkaisuja M 65, Tampere.

Heikkinen, Jorma (1986), *Vanhainkotiasukkaan terveydentila ja ennuste*, Tutkimus vuosina 1970, 1975 ja 1980 Tampereen kaupungin vanhainkotiin tulleiden henkilöiden elinoloista ja terveydentilasta sekä selviytymisestä vanhainkodissa viiden vuoden seuranta-aikana, Tampereen yliopisto, Acta Universitatis Tamperensis Ser A Vol 215, Tampere.

Jylhä, Marja (1985), *Oman terveyden kokeminen eläkeiässä*, Tampereen yliopisto, Acta Universitatis Tamperensis Ser A Vol 195, Tampere.

Jylhä, Marja (1990), 'Terveys ja sairaus', in Pohjolainen, Pertti & Jylhä, Marja (eds.) (1990), *Vanheneminen ja elämänkulku. Sosiaaligerontologian perusteita*, Weilin+Göös, Espoo.

Jyrkämä, Jyrki & Randell, Seppo (1987), *Vanheneminen ja yhteiskunta. Vanhuuden ja vanhenemisen tarkastelua suomalaisen sosiaaligerontologisen tutkimuksen pohjalta*, Tampereen yliopisto, Sosiologian ja sosiaalipsykologian laitoksen sarja B, työraportteja 23, Tampere.

Kansaneläkelaitos (1990), *Tilasto Suomen eläkkeensaajista*, Kansaneläke- ja työeläkerekistereihin perustuva tilastollinen vuosikirja (1989), Eläketurvakeskus, Kansaneläkelaitos, Helsinki.

Klaukka, Timo (1982), 'Aikuisten terveydentila ja hoidon tarve', in *Terveyspalvelusten tarve, käyttö ja kustannukset 1964-1976*, Kansaneläkelaitoksen julkaisuja A 18, Kansaneläkelaitos, Helsinki.

Koskiaho, Briitta (1986), *Elämänmuoto ja perusparantaminen. Esimerkki asumisesta vanhoilla asuinalueilla entisinä aikoina ja nyt*, Tampereen yliopisto, Sosiaalipolitiikan laitos, tutkimuksia 78, Tampere.

Koskiaho, Briitta (1987), *Ikääntyminen ja asuminen. Uusien asumisratkaisujen etsimistä*, Vellamonkatu 15, Tampere.

Lilja, Reija & Santamäki-Vuori, Tuire & Standing, Guy (1990), *Työttömyys ja työmarkkinoiden joustavuus Suomessa*, Työpoliittinen tutkimus 6, Työministeriö, Helsinki.

Luokkala, Anni (1987), *Tamperelaisten 75 vuotta täyttäneiden asunto-olot ja palvelutarpeet*, Tampereen kaupungin tutkimuksia ja selvityksiä 60, Tampereen kaupungin sosiaalikeskus, Tampere.

Pättiniemi, Maija-Liisa (1989), *'Pumpulin plikan'* elämä. *Vanhainkodissa asuvien entisten Finlaysonin naistyöntekijöiden elämäntapa prosessina elämäkertojen perusteella*, Tampereen yliopisto, Sosiaalipolitiikan laitos, pro gradu -tutkielma, Tampere.

Ronkainen, Suvi (1990), *Ikääntyvän naisen seksuaalisuus. Ikääntymisen vaikutus naisen seksuaalielämään elämänhistorian valossa*, Tasa-arvojulkaisuja, sarja D, Naistutkimusraportteja 1, Sosiaali- ja terveysministeriö, Helsinki.

Sauli, Hannele et al. (1989), 'Elinolot numeroina, Vuoden 1986 elinolotutkimus', *Elinolot* 1989:1, Tilastokeskus, Helsinki.

Sipilä, Jorma (1979), *Sosiaalisten ongelmien synty ja lievittäminen*, Tammi, Helsinki.

Sneck, Timo et al. (1987), *Tampereen vanhustenhuoltoverkoston kehittämismahdollisuudet skenaariomuodossa*, Tampereen kaupungin tutkimuksia ja selvityksiä 59, Valtion teknillinen tutkimuskeskus, Yhdyskunta- ja rakennesuunnittelun laboratorio, Tampere.

Sosiaalihallitus (1988), *Kunnan vanhustenhuolto sosiaali- ja terveydenhuollon yhteistyönä*, Sosiaalihallitus, opas 2/1988 (Lääkintöhallituksen opassarja 3), Helsinki.

Suomen tilastollinen vuosikirja (STV) (1990), Tilastokeskus, Helsinki.

Tampereen kaupungin asunto-ohjelma 1990-1994 (1990), Tampereen kaupungin tutkimuksia ja selvityksiä 76, Tampereen kaupunki, Tilastotoimisto, Tampere.

Tampereen kaupungin sosiaalikeskus (1988), *Turvalliseen vanhuuteen. Tampereen vanhustenhuollon kehittämisohjelma vuoteen 2000*, Tampereen kaupungin tutkimuksia ja selvityksiä 67, Tampereen kaupungin sosiaalikeskus, Tampere.

Tampereen väestö 1990. Ikäryhmittäiset ja osa-alueittaiset tilastot (1990), Tampereen kaupunki, Tilastotoimisto, Kuntasuunnittelun perustilastoja 39, Tampere.

Uusitalo, Hannu (STAKES), Interview 2 October 1991.

Valkonen, Tapani & Nikander, Timo (1990), 'Vanhojen ikäluokkien koon ja rakenteen muutokset', in Pohjolainen, Pertti & Jylhä, Marja (eds.) (1990), *Vanheneminen ja elämänkulku. Sosiaaligerontologian perusteita*, Weilin+Göös, Espoo.

Virta, Kari & Toivola, Matti (1993), *Sosiaaliturvan pääpiirteet*. Helsinki.

Vähämäki, Eeva (1990), *Yksityinen vaiko kunnallinen*, Vertailututkimus yksityisen ja kunnallisen palvelukeskuksen yhteydessä, omissa asunnoissaan asuvien, yli 75-vuotiaiden iäkkäiden hyvinvoinnista haastattelujen perusteella, Tampereen yliopisto, Sosiaalipolitiikan laitos, pro gradu -tutkielma, Tampere.

Part Two
JAPAN

5 Japanese women in their society

Briitta Koskiaho

This is an intertextual analysis of Japanese women. As material I have used texts written by Western researchers, as well as texts from Japanese studies and statistical material collected by public authorities. Different narratives of the Japanese society define the role and position of women from their own national viewpoint. When Western evaluators discuss the position of the Japanese women, they frequently adopt a very critical approach. The Japanese themselves, in turn, understand the role of females against the history and traditions of their own society and culture.

Some years ago the postmodern direction in Western research made it possible to use different research approaches at the same time, thus legitimizing them from a scientific viewpoint (Fraser & Nicholson 1988, 373-394). Different narratives of social processes are just stories; no absolute or pure truth exists. Different stories of the same object enable us to understand the reality as a complex whole (Eco 1981).

The narratives related to the long common history of the Japanese people, with their emphasis on common inherited values and patterns of behaviour, have strongly influenced the consciousness of the Japanese people. The position and role of women have to be understood against this mythical background. Another approach is to see the women in Japan from the perspective of the dominant role of the economy. When the economy has needed labour, women have been allowed to enter working life. If, on the other hand, the economy has needed women to support the men, the women have stayed at home. At the same time women have been exploited as sexual objects either in prostitution or by more sophisticated methods as barmaids, show girls or traditionally as geishas. A third way to understand the position of women in Japan is to see them as parties to a contract — a sexual or gender contract (Pateman 1988). Women have a very clear role in the social system and have themselves participated in the process of shaping their own position and role in society. This is a cultural explanation. The contract ensures the women some benefits but at the same time places certain demands on them. For example, they have to produce various services to their family and at the same time indirectly assist the whole social system. The contract view easily turns into a deterministic explanation.

Two parallel processes are taking place in Japan today. One is a change in the female life model and the other is a new demand for a highly educated female workforce. The women's attitudes towards their role and position in society are changing, beginning with the highly educated segments of women and spreading to other groups. The economy, too, needs to see the female workforce as a real alternative for different occupations, including the male sector of working life.

In East Asia, public life has traditionally been masculine. Consequently, all public organizations and forms of social life centre around the interests of men. The women have their own semipublic networks, mostly related to their activities as house-wives and therefore centred around the house and home life. From a historical perspective, the strong women's movement and its different orientations since the beginning of this century represent a new phenomenon.

In the following I shall focus on the home-oriented life of housewives and their changing role in the labour market and working life. Working life constitutes a central question, because the Japanese society is very work-centred. This main area is masculine in character, even though most Japanese women participate in paid employment in some phase of their lives. However, they do not work permanently like men. In fact, it is the women who make it possible for men to work as worker ants. Who takes care of the home, the intimate world of life? The woman, naturally. In conclusion I shall discuss the problem of distinguishing between Eastern and Western cultural elements.

The Japanese housewife as an institution —
Housewife as a profession

The average life expectancy at birth for Japanese women was 47 years in 1930 and 82 years in 1990, the highest in the world. Correspondingly, life expectancy for men in 1990 was 76 years, which is also the highest in the world. The number of children a woman bears in her lifetime decreased from an average of 4.1 in 1940 to 1.7 in 1987. In 1985, when her youngest child started school, the mother was in average 35.5 years old. She could then expect to live 46 more years. When her youngest child got married, the mother was 56, and could still expect to live 18 more years until the death of her husband. She became widow at the age of 74 years (Japanese Working Life Profile 1988; Women Workers in Japan 1988).

In their late thirties, married women begin to have more free time. This middle age lasts nearly 20 years. In their old age they spend nearly 18 years just with the husband. How to spend these free years of life, is a widely discussed topic in Japan. The divorce rate in Japan is growing, but is not nearly so high as in the Western countries. The annual divorce rate per 1,000 mid-year population in Japan was 1.3 in 1989, compared with 4.8 in the U.S.A., 4.8 in the UK and 2.2 in Sweden. The great majority of Japanese women still follow the above pattern in their lives.

Quite often women choose to marry and work until the birth of their first child. Nowadays, because of the low birth rate, the wives may enjoy a fairly long period of free time from about their mid-forties till their mid-fifties, when their husbands retire. If the wife is at home and if she can afford it, she will go in for various activities outside the home. She may attend study groups, do charitable work or participate in other community activities. On the other hand, she may also return to paid employment, often to a part-time job or temporary employment.

When a woman gets married and has children, she is expected to act as a professional housewife (Imamura 1988, 73-97; Women of Japan). This role demands the same degree of commitment as her husband gives to his work. Although the wife may combine other roles with motherhood and caring, she cannot allow them to compete with her maternal role. The profession of the Japanese housewife includes managing the family finances, taking care of the husband when he is at home, being more or less totally responsible for the children, and caring for the husband's old parents, if they are living in the same household. A very important part of the role of the housewife is to see to it that the children do well in the extremely competitive school entrance examinations. This means after-school tutoring and prep schools. The professional housewife participates in the Parent Teacher Associations in order to keep up with relevant information and to convince the teachers that she really takes her children's education seriously.

She also has to maintain a good image in the neighbourhood. This is particularly important, if the family expects to reside there until their children get married. Especially in the case of a daughter, the family of the future husband may want to investigate the background of their daughter-in-law and her family by asking the neighbours to vouch for the family character before marriage agreements are made. After the children have left home, the housewife takes on the role of the carer of her retired husband or the aged parents of her husband.

This picture of the housewife also involves a series of obligations which keep her close to the home. She chooses her work and other activities with care so that she can do them in the time she has free from her responsibilities as wife and mother. This limits her to activities which are close to the home and can be done in short periods of time, or started and dropped, as she moves through the different stages in her life course.

The young generations question this model of the housewife dating back to the 1920s and 1930s. Their ideals are changing. Younger women like to be free and try to avoid an early marriage. Living as a single woman has been an almost unknown lifestyle in Japan until recently.

Housing and home-centred life

Japan has urbanized very rapidly after the Second World War. Her urban population increased from 25 per cent in 1930 to 68 per cent in 1980. As a consequence, provision of adequate housing constitutes a severe problem, especially in the metropolitan areas of Tokyo, Kyoto, Osaka, Kobe and Nagoya, where half of the whole population live. In addition, land prices have risen sharply in large cities since the 1960s. If we mark the level of land price in 1955 by

100, the index was 21,002 in 1991 (Japan 1992, An International Comparison 1992).

Compared with the other industrialized countries, Japanese dwellings are small and expensive. As in Finland, people in Japan like to own their homes. The ownership ratio is more than 60 per cent. Privately rented flats are the least desirable category of housing. Five different types of housing are common in urban areas: privately owned homes, condominiums (blocks of flats in which the residents may purchase housing units comprising a single room or more), company housing, public housing and privately rented flats (Imamura 1988, 73-97).

Other housing forms than public housing and privately owned housing are typical of young families or single dwellers. Middle-aged and elderly residents mostly live in their own houses or in public housing units. Dwellers with smaller incomes live in public housing and privately rented flats. The average educational level is the highest for houseowners or condominium dwellers. This means that middle-aged white-collar workers can afford their own house, but young professionals who are only starting their careers live in their own small dwellings, are often single and typically commuters, working temporarily in another town. This is a very common phenomenon in the Japanese working life.

Different housing forms also mean differentiated housing circles (Nozawa & Takahashi 1990). The world of the housewife consists of the private house and its area, occupied by the owner. Spiritually or mentally, the distance between these areas and privately rented housing areas is the greatest. According to a large empirical study of housewives in greater Tokyo, if both types of housing are to be found in the same neighbourhood with only one Parent-Teacher Association, people from different housing categories do not meet or know each other (Imamura 1988, 73-97). In small towns people know each other better and this might help in communications.[1]

Life in rented flats seemed to be very private. The women did not visit each other, while the wives living in owner occupied houses formed a very closed community. One practical aspect which differentiated the women in rented houses from each other was paid work. The women worked part time or did piecework. Women of rented housing quarters assembled radio parts at home for a nearby factory.

The attitudes of women living in their own homes were quite

harsh: they shared a lack of understanding of the strange people in their neighbourhood who did not live in their own homes and did not engage in volunteer work and other community activities. Women living in their own houses had the resources to participate in all kinds of activities. They believed the others only thought about the needs of their own families. The interpretation of the researcher, however, was that this group was suffering from apathy and powerlessness.

Women living in company houses regarded their housing as temporary and tried to be polite to each other, but to keep a distance at the same time, so that their husbands would not have any trouble from their housing. Such trouble could influence the work situation and the husband could lose face, which is the worst thing that can happen in Japan. The whole family had to behave in a proper manner. These women were wary of close involvements because the residents had the highest degree of mutual visibility. They tried to seek their friends and contacts from outside the housing area. They moved their sphere of activity outside where there was less visibility. Acting in the housing community reflected the primacy of the husband's needs at work. The women were careful not to ask for any services from the other dwellers because these were either in a position above or below them, depending on the position of their husbands. Those above could not be asked to do any favours, while those below would have had difficulty in refusing.

Many women living in company houses were faced with constant uncertainty about being transferred to another town. They had already moved a great deal. For such women, outside work was difficult, unless they had specific skills. There were part-time jobs in the neighbourhood stores, for example, but the women who expected to move at any moment tended to put off looking for a job.

Women in detached private houses and condominiums were more likely to be concerned about neighbourhood relations than women in other housing categories. The only exceptions were some women in privately rented houses, who had settled permanently. A major motive of this neighbourhood concern was the children's welfare. In other studies of the Tokyo neighbourhoods, the community feelings and activities of women centred around school and the children (Bestor 1989; Family and Community in Japan 1986).

100

The degree to which these women were motivated to participate in various activities varies according to their age. Older women who had just moved into condominiums were looking for friends. Younger women made friends through their children's kindergartens and either joined 'circles' together or formed them in order to make more permanent friends. They participated in activities for many years and found lasting friends. The women in their own houses were concerned about maintaining good neighbourly relations for their children, and as they grew older they stressed the importance of good long-term relationships.

In the countryside, relations are mostly family to family directed, while the urban contacts of females are mostly centred around their children. When the children grow up, many women lose the main basis of their contacts. Especially if people have to move to a new neighbourhood after their children are grown up, they lack the support of long-term relations which they had in the countryside. At any rate, the older women much prefer such long-term relationships.

The life circles of females and males differ significantly in Japan. For females, especially for wives, the urban neighbourhood comes close to community: all the significant activities of life take place there. Especially, people living in their own houses emphasize their neighbourhood. Men spend their lives mostly outside the neighbourhood and its significance to them is not so important. The life of women is more home-centred and the life of men work-centred. The contacts and networks arise from different sources according to gender.

Women in working life

Traditionally work in rural society had to do with agriculture and fishing and women were also involved in these. According to the Population Census, as late as 1950 the number of women engaged in primary industries accounted for more than 60 per cent of employed women, but this rate dropped to 10 per cent in 1985. The Labour Force Survey gives a much lower rate, because the classification of rural women is different by farmers' wives and family members. The same problem has been pointed out in Finland. (Japanese Working Life Profile 1988, and 1993-1994;

Working Women in Japan 1989.)

The majority of factory workers in the first decades of the Meiji-period were women and children. Manufacturing was mostly light industry. Especially textile manufacturing declined and was substituted by heavy industry, which uses male labour. At the same time the housewife ideology gained in popularity and, consequently, the main task of a real wife was to rear good new citizens for the nation. After the war the housewife ideology remained dominant in the middle class: for women it meant serving their hard working men, taking care of their children and the aged parents of their husbands, but no work outside the home. The social welfare system was undeveloped and could remain that way because of the housewife's role.

The housewife ideology has also meant a partly hidden matriarchy with many housewife associations and networks as a compensation for the networks of work, which belong to the world of men. In the golden age of housewife ideology (in 1967), 63 per cent of women were members of female organizations.

During the remarkable economic progress in the 1960s there was an increased demand for labour and the shortage of manpower constituted an acute problem, resulting in the recognition of women as members of the labour force. Still the female labour remained secondary in importance compared with the male. Women started working again, but now in many cases as part-timers or by combining domestic and paid work at home.

Table 1
Female employment structure by marital status
(non-agriculture), per cent

	Unmarried	Married	Widowed, divorced	Total
1960	55.2	32.7	12.0	100.0
1975	38.0	51.3	10.8	100.0
1985	31.8	58.8	9.4	100.0
1992	33.1	57.6	9.2	100.0

Source: Working Women in Japan 1989; Japanese Working Life Profile 1993-1994

In 1960 more than half of the working women were unmarried, and 12 per cent were divorced or widowed, while thirty years later almost 60 per cent were married and more than half of married women were working (57.6 per cent are married in non-agricultural female labour (1992)).

During the period following the two oil crises, when the great boom of the Japanese economy came to an end and the rapid economic growth turned to a more even growth, the main change involved technological innovation and a service-oriented economy. Women's labour experienced a qualitative change. The introduction of new technology, especially electronics, greatly reduced hard physical labour and eliminated barriers between men and women in the production sector. The jobs of men and women, however, are still different at the work place.

Until the 1970s, the Japanese economy was largely based on manufacturing although service industries have steadily grown in importance. The economy was based on dual labour market, on the seniority of male employees and on the part-time work of female workers, as well as on casual male workers often employed by subcontractors who cannot offer the same job security as the larger companies to their permanent male employees. Routine clerical, service or assembly work has been carried out by casual, part-time or temporary workers.

Table 2
Female labour by industry in 1960–1988, per cent

	Primary industry	Secondary industry	Tertiary industry	Total
1960	43	20	37	100
1970	26	26	48	100
1975	18	26	56	100
1985	11	28	61	100
1988	10	27	63	100
1988 male	7	38	55	100

Source: Women Workers in Japan 1988

In 1960, almost half of the female employees worked in primary industries, while in 1988 they accounted for 10 per cent. In the tertiary sector, the number of female workers has increased relatively more than that of male workers. However, labour in the secondary industry has not diminished; on the contrary, it has grown from the year 1960.

In the total workforce, the distribution of labour in different industries follows the same pattern as in the Western industrialized countries: 6 per cent in primary, 34 per cent in secondary, and 60 per cent in tertiary sector (1993) (Japanese Working Life Profile 1993-1994).

The Japanese researchers estimate that office automation has expanded opportunities irrespective of sex and has opened new opportunities and fields of activity for women. Still the rate of employment of women in technical and managerial occupations is very small. The gradual increase in services connected to caring has resulted in new employment opportunities for women.

Table 3
The employment status of females by occupation in 1960–1988, per cent

	1960	1975	1980	1988	1992
Professional & technical work	9.0	11.6	13.7	14.1	13.7
Administration work	0.3	0.9	0.9	1.0	1.0
Clerical work	25.4	32.2	33.0	33.3	34.9
Sales	8.7	11.1	12.1	12.7	12.7
Agriculture & forestry & fishery	3.6	0.8	0.7	0.6	0.6
Mining	0.7	0.0	0.0	0.0	0.0
Transport & communication	0.3	1.5	0.7	0.6	0.5
Skilled workers, production process workers, labourers	35.9	28.3	27.4	26.7	25.1
Maintenance and services	16.1	13.7	11.3	10.9	11.2
Total	100.0	100.0	100.0	100.0	100.0

Source: Labour Force Survey, Working Women in Japan 1989; Japanese Working Life Profile 1993-94

One third of all female employees work as secretaries or in other clerical work, and one fourth in industrial production. 11-13 per cent are occupied as professional and technical workers, as sales workers, and as protective service workers and service workers. Only one per cent are working on the managerial level, five per cent as manual workers, and less than one per cent in farming, fishing or forestry.

In terms of occupations, the rate of women in technical and managerial work is the highest among physicians and dentists (11 per cent), the lowest among heads of schools (0.3-2.3 per cent) and civil servants in managerial positions (1.4 per cent).

The occupational areas which showed the greatest growth rate among women in the period from 1970 to 1985 were sports, information processing, social welfare, and the arts and writing, all significantly different from the traditional female professions. Women have also entered other fields previously dominated by men, such as the natural sciences.

The rate of long-term female workers who had worked continuously for ten years or more nearly doubled from 13 per cent to 25 per cent in the period of 1970-1985, the rise being especially conspicuous in the age group of those in their twenties. This indicates that an increasing number of women stay on in the labour market after marriage and pregnancy. Part-time employment has also increased, especially in the service sector. From the whole workforce the rate of part-timers is 13 per cent (1991). There are two types of part-time work in Japan: the old type developed in the manufacturing industry and the new one in the service sector. The old type consists of simple and repetitive work for females at lower wages than those earned by regular workers. The new type is coupled with the tertiary industry's increasing demand for part-timers during the busy hours of business. The rate of part-timers in the whole female labour increased from 9 per cent in 1960 to 12 per cent in 1970, reaching 22 per cent in 1985 and 31 per cent in 1992. The majority of part-timers (63 per cent) work in services, while the second largest group works in manufacturing (21 per cent).

With the spread of office automation, increasing attention has been paid to work which is done at home instead of offices, and to the future of such work. From the beginning of the Meiji-period housewives have traditionally worked at home for nearby factories. In many slum areas, situated near match factories, women used to work at home packing matches into boxes. The work was dangerous because of the risk of phosphorus contamination.

Female occupations in which at least 70 per cent of the workers are women (Women Workers in Japan 1988; Women's Occupation Careers in Japan 1988):

— in professional and technical occupations: nutritionists, nurses and kindergarten teachers
— clerical and related employees
— in sales jobs: insurance agents and canvassers
— in transportation and communications: telephone operators
— in crafts, process production and manual work: light industry workers
— in services: domestic and other servants, beauticians, waitresses, barmaids, cabaret waitresses, geishas, dancehall girls and advertising employees.

Primary industries are excluded from the above list.

The main trends have been: an increase of female labour in the tertiary sector, with an expanding range of employment; longer terms of service; an increase of part-timers in the tertiary sector; and the emergence of temporary workers and at-home workers.

Textile girls in the Meiji-period were very young. They stopped working in their early twenties. Since then the main part of female labour has been very young, but in recent years the number of employees aged 35 years or over has gradually risen. At the same time the rate of employment among married women has increased. The participation rate has grown especially in the young female groups, among women aged 20-24 years and 25-29 years. The age group of 30-34 years has the lowest rate. There are two peaks, one in the age group of 20-24 years and the other in the age group of 45-49 years. More than seventy per cent of women in these age groups are already in working life.

Young females start working after school and continue to work for two or three years. After marriage most wives remain at home for a number of years. They start working again later to earn money for their children's prep school or for other economical reasons. At this stage, however, they can no longer get permanent jobs.

106

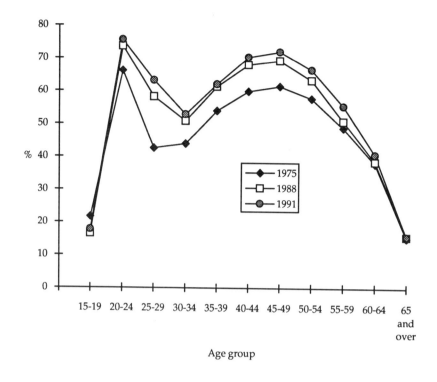

Figure 1   Female labour force participation rate by age group

Source: Women Workers in Japan 1988; Japanese Working Life
Profile 1993-1994

The employer has traditionally benefited from the two-peak model: it has consisted of unskilled and cheap female workforce, as well as of the low-cost welfare system. The label of part-timer has served the ideological purposes of devaluing the female labour force rather than described accurately the working conditions of women. The part-time and temporary working model as a general employment pattern means that women are not taken seriously by employers. They are only regarded as part of the reserve army of labour. The working hours of part-timers, however, are almost the same as in full-time jobs in Finland. One average part-timer works 33 hours in a five and half day week. Although the part-timers

107

work hard and long hours, they are still outsiders in working life. Social security benefits of the enterprise or trade unions are not available to women employees. They do not belong to the essential company members and are not included in the company community or baptised into the company culture. Females are outsiders, they do not fit in the seniority system or the company *ie*-like atmosphere (Berentsen 1985, 17-20). Women work for money. Their real life happens outside the work place, while to men it is the company that represents their real life.[2]

Participation of women in working life after they have reached retirement age is quite extensive in Japan. Nearly one third of women between 65-69 years continue to work, while 18 per cent of 70-74-year-olds and 7 per cent of those over 75 years still work.

The main source of household finance comes from the work of the husband; the salary of the wife is secondary. The salary level for women is about 40 per cent below the level of salaries for men. According to a study of wage differences made by the Ministry of Labour, the wage gap between men and women is the biggest in the age group of 45-49 years. In this group the women earn about 70 per cent of the wage level of men. This age group represents one of the peaks of the working curve for women. Many women work at this age. The comparison only includes regular workers in enterprises; they have started working for their company after graduation and continue to work for the same enterprise. Several factors differentiate the wage level between men and women: the seniority system favours men; women give up their work when they get married and have children; industries which employ female workers often pay low salaries (many of these work places are small companies where the wage level is low); there is disparity in the academic background of men and women; and a quarter women employees do part-time work.

It should also be noted that the Japanese wage system provides various forms of allowances, such as allowances for dependent family (paid to male workers) and housing. These benefits are mostly made available to the male heads of family only.

In 1976, the Prime Minister's Office did a survey on the attitudes of the different sexes towards the position of women (Women of Japan). Attitudes towards women staying at home were directly related to age. In the young generation (20-29 years), 40 per cent of women were against the traditional role of females, while in the eldest group aged 70 years or over, 61 per cent were for it. Among men, traditionalism was deeply rooted. Among the youngest men, only 30 per cent were against the traditional role, while among the eldest 73 per cent were for it.

According to a survey from 1987, 47 per cent of women wanted to raise their children themselves and to take on a job again after they were free from family responsibilities (Working Women of Japan 1989, 25). The attitudes seemed to be connected with social allowances. If child care allowances had been available, 36 per cent would have liked to continue working after having a child. According to a survey from 1983, in the real situation, without any assistance, only 17 per cent preferred to work. The state controls the conduct, attitudes and will of people by means of its social policy. In 1987, 19 per cent of women wanted to stay at home after marriage and 16 per cent wanted to take on a permanent job.

The educational system has had its own impact on women's attitudes towards a career. The traditional diversification of the educational system after senior secondary school has led girls to go to a special training school, like nursing school, or a so-called short university (*tanki daigaku*), junior college, or women's university (*joshi daigaku*). Only a small proportion of women have opted for an ordinary university course (*sôgo daigaku* or *byogaun daigaku*). Consequently, the attitudes of men and women towards work already begin to diverge during their educational years (Teichler 1973, 169-187).

In 1979, only one half of women students in universities expected to stay in paid work for more than ten years, while 80 per cent of women students in short universities were of the opinion that they could not stay in paid work for more than ten years. The women's universities have been criticized for cultivating all sorts of unnecessary components in their curricula, while they at the same time neglect the really essential aspects of university education.

Education in these places did not prepare the girls to become active individuals who would pursue real academic studies. The gender differentiated educational system thus prepared females and males for differentiated tasks in society. In 1980, 60 per cent of short university graduates entered office work, 34 per cent entered clerical work, and 29 per cent went to public services, such as social work (Slawik 1981).

In 1984, 20 per cent of junior secondary school women graduates and 24 per cent of college and university graduates thought they would like to continue working even after marriage and pregnancy. Correspondingly, 45 per cent of junior secondary school women graduates and 52 per cent of university graduates said they would prefer to leave working life temporarily after marriage and pregnancy and return to work after raising their children. Those with a lower education more often wanted to remain at home as housewives than those with a higher educational level. The preferences between 1979 and 1984 changed slowly from a pure housewife career to a double career model.

Table 4
Trends in occupational composition of female graduates from 4-year university

	1975	1980	1985	1991	1992
Total	42,437	61,558	66,890	98,582	103,082
Composition ratio by occupation	100.0	100.0	100.0	100.0	100.0
Professional and technical workers	52.7	55.9	50.5	42.3	39.5
Engineers	3.4	4.0	10.5	15.0	14.7
School teachers	38.1	37.5	27.4	17.0	15.0
Workers in health and medical care occupations	7.1	7.9	6.8	5.2	4.8
Others	4.1	6.6	5.8	5.2	5.0
Clerical and related workers	40.4	36.6	39.1	45.3	47.0
Sales workers	3.1	5.1	7.8	9.6	10.0
Others	3.8	2.4	2.5	2.9	3.6

Source: Ministry of Education, Basic Survey on Schools (Japan Labor Bulletin, September 1, 1994)

The trends in the occupational composition of female graduates referred to above indicate that in reality the career opportunities of women have not improved. In fact, in the 1990s women with academic qualifications have more often than before, or in half of all cases, been obliged to start their careers with secretarial duties.

Extension of female working life

Like in Europe, the old manufacturing industries in Japan have undergone extensive restructuring since the late 1970s. The Japanese economy can no longer be understood without reference to Southeastern Asia. The cheap production costs, as labour costs, in these countries provide advantages to the Japanese capital.

Many labour and energy intensive industries, as well as polluting industries, have moved out. Electronics and textile industries are good examples. When new jobs for women develop in the tertiary sector in Japan, manufacturing gives work to Southeastern Asian women in their home countries, as it used to give to young Japanese women before the Second World War. At that time Japanese women formed the majority of the whole workforce in manufacturing.

In recent years the feminist theorists have analysed the ways in which women's labour is integrated into the global economy and the international division of labour. Research and development, as well as processes that are capital and technology intensive, are carried out in the developed countries, while labour intensive processes are realized in the Third World. These processes take advantage of the cheap female labour.

Another question concerning the use of labour is the exploitation of sexuality. The women's movement in Japan has been greatly concerned about prostitution which has been seen as a social problem. Rural young women in the Meiji period moved from the country into towns to work as 'textile girls'. Many of them did not return home after giving up their work in the mill. They preferred to stay in town, but lacked any real possibilities of earning their livelihood in a respectable manner if they did not marry. Many girls ended up as prostitutes (Saxonhouse 1976, 97-125).

Several writers see links between the earlier 'Yoshiwara' quarters in Japan and a recent phenomenon, sex tours by Japanese men to Southeastern Asian countries. This type of tourism became extremely popular in Japan in the prosperous 1970s and 1980s. Similarly, women from Southeast Asia have been transported to Japan to work as barmaids and prostitutes in the redlight districts of cities (McCormack & Sugimato 1988).[3] Many women in Southeastern Asian countries are working in various sex services and tourist industry. It has been estimated that 40-75 per cent of the profit made in this industry goes back to the country of the owner of the hotel or travel agency. In tourist areas, the bars are frequently owned by foreigners, and a significant number of the owners are Japanese or Australian. Japanese men have readily used the services of the tourist and prostitution industry in the neighbour countries, and the economic profits have gone back home. It can be noted therefore that it is not only the manufacturing industry using female labour that has moved its production out of Japan. A large part of the prostitution industry has done the same. Women's sexuality has thus been the accumulator of foreign exchange and capital.

The women in Southeastern Asia have participated in the industrialization of their societies as manufacturing workers. They have also become the objects of the prostitution industry. Compared with the earlier Meiji period in Japan, the process of industrialization in Southeastern Asia over the last decades is quite different, however. In the Meiji period, the Japanese society defined its own activities, but in the case of Southeastern Asia the dominators come from outside, from Japan for example. Female labour has been crudely exploited in both cases, in the industrializing Japan last century and in the present-day Southeastern Asia. In this connection, the Meiji textile mills and the electronic industry in Southeastern Asia are comparable, even if the time is different.

Towards a new understanding of gender relations

Japanese feminism has long traditions. The first wave occurred at the beginning of this century, and the second powerful wave arrived in the 1970s. The first tended to confine itself to the movement for women's rights and the second one questioned the sex-role division itself. Women have been very active in other civil rights movements, such as anti-pollution or anti-nuclear movements (Women of Japan; Refsing 1990; Linhart, R. 1986, 216-232; Kato 1988, 232-234).

As part-time working has expanded, women have learnt that working outside the home does not liberate them. Before they started working, it seemed as if work might solve all their problems, but this has not been a realistic view. According to one interpretation, women have been exploited both inside and outside their homes. Feminism has come to face a contradiction: If the dual role oppresses the women more than before, should they stay at home? One faction in the women's movement emphasizes the role of the home as a liberating shelter from capitalistic oppression. This attitude used to be common among the political right wing, now it is expressed by the left wing. For women, equality means acceptance of male standards in working conditions, such as overtime, frequent business trips, and the possibility of transfer. Conversely, the protection of women means a lower status compared with men, part-time work without social security as an employee, and/or domestic work.

The same contradiction also prevails in the West, but in the East combining working life and home life is still harder for women who want to make a career. It has been estimated that the Law on Equal Employment Opportunities from the year 1986 only widened the polarisation between career women, housewives and part-timers. The women's movement in Japan demands both equality and protection, instead of either equality or protection. Part-time work has been used as an excuse to utilize women's labour at a lower cost. Equality at the cost of protection will end up in reinforcing the exploitation of women's labour.

The Japanese women's movement seems to conflict with the Equality Law. The members insist that protection should be extended to male workers and not be used as an excuse for keeping women's wages low. Men should reduce their hours of work and share the housekeeping and child rearing duties more equally with their wives. Women have traditionally specialized in home making, as well as in building and maintaining the local community. In the 1990s, the women's movement is inviting men to accept child rearing responsibilities, which is quite extraordinary in the Japanese context. Women are entering the public world and men the home. Some new legislative innovations have already emerged concerning the care of children.

Many big companies have begun to provide new social services which their female employees cannot get from the public sector, as they can in Finland. Some department stores, for example, hold the jobs open for mothers who take a few years off to raise their children. Companies may run 'babysitter hotline' nurseries for working mothers who need child care in an emergency situation.

113

Some firms are experimenting with flexitime in their offices. The giant business firms are in fact pioneers in the development of social services for females (Solo 1989, 64-68).

This strategy is exceptional in view of the former polarisation of the two worlds. Women have gained power by stressing their difference from men, as well as by emphasizing their status as the boss in the management of the family. After all, it is the women who are in charge of the family budget and the husband's whole salary. In the past, the same wives spent more time and shared more experiences with other women than with their husbands. This sisterhood of housewives has been a powerful factor in society. In a sense, it has meant a liberating resource for women compared with men who spend all their time on business duties. The situation already causes serious health problems to the overworked men, resulting in exhaustion, the *karôshi* phenomenon.

The Japanese women have traditionally taken care of their parents-in-law, but the feminists now require men to take care of their own parents. Some male-dominated labour unions have even demanded a paid leave for their members who care for their aged parents, which some time ago would have been inconceivable.

The majority of Japanese men are simply breadwinners for their families. They have no status in the home. The average life expectancy for women and men in Japan is high. More and more men will live on at home after retirement in the future. This is a totally new situation. In the countryside, men and women used to work in agriculture for as long as they lived; there never came a time when they could have just sat down to enjoy a restful life at home. In urban occupations, in contrast, more and more Japanese men, having worked all their lives and having reached an old age, will come back home in a new sense. They will have to find new ways of participating in the family activities which have always been quite distant to them.

What will happen to those young women who want to participate in the masculine working life as career makers? The 1980s saw the emergence of a new type of female, still partly postmodern and partly traditional. The proportion of women in professional or technical work increased in 1960-1980 (in 1960 9%, in 1980 14%) at the same time as the proportion of women factory workers declined (in 1960 36%, in 1980 5%). By ILO definitions (1991), more than 40 per cent of the entire workforce are women, including young girls aged 15-19; the majority of the latter are schoolgirls or students (Women Workers in Japan 1988; Japanese Working Life Profile 1993-94).

Table 5
Change in the number of female managerial workers, females/all managerial workers in 1970 and 1985, per cent

Occupation	1970	1985
Government officials	1.0	1.4
Directors of companies and corporations	8.2	12.2
Other managers and administrators	1.3	1.7
Total	4.6	8.5

Source: Women Workers in Japan 1988

The total number of managers and administrators in decision-making positions more than doubled from 1970 to 1985, with a 10 per cent increase in the total number of female workers.

In the 1980s, the old tradition of dividing the new female employees into two categories within the company began to change. From 1982 to 1987, the number of women in managerial positions increased by 50 per cent. One of the old categories was related to managerial positions and was male by nature, while the other was female and led to clerical work and tea serving. From the end of the 1980s, large numbers of college-educated women have for the first time been set on the managerial track. This revolutionary practice is based on an economic necessity, not an ideology. The demand for labour in the booming economy of the 1980s outstripped the supply. The shortage of labour penetrated the whole economy but was especially acute in the rapidly growing high-technology sector. How to train and utilize female labour is one of the biggest issues for Japanese companies today.

At the same time the new female generation changed its attitudes towards work compared with older generations. Until recently, most women did not want to make a career for themselves, and companies overlooked the few who did so. In practice, however, the position of career women has not been very clear in the work places, as can be seen from the following story (Solo 1989, 64-68; Fornander 1990, 61-66):

> Early each morning for a week at a time, K. S. arrives at Toshiba's headquarters in Tokyo to dust the tops of her colleagues' desks. It is a duty shared by the 15 women who work among the 19 men in one of the company's electronic components sales group. She cannot imagine men doing it. She is not a subservient Office Lady, however. She has a degree from Tokyo University and has ambitions which most Office Ladies could never conceive. She expects to be a manager in an overseas office. She has studied philosophy for a year in France and hopes to work there one day. In 1989 Toshiba had only ten women among its 7,000 managers, but according to company estimates, there will be hundreds of women managers within a decade.

A governmental research report on the situation of women workers in 1988 gives a very positive evaluation of the recent progress of women in working life. The report concludes, however, that so far the pace of progress has been slow and that the present situation cannot be considered satisfactory bearing in mind that women represent 40 per cent of all workers. In the future, the situation is expected to improve, the number of women employees with long years of service will increase, and the range of occupations in which women work will expand. 'When the expression 'the first woman' no longer has any news value, true equality has begun.' (Women Workers in Japan 1988, 67.)

In the early 1990s the economic situation changed in a negative direction, which can mean a temporary or an ongoing break in the liberation of female career opportunities.

The East and the West

Many Japanese researchers stress the special character of Asian cultures. Modernization is a product of Western culture, and industrialization is not necessarily part of it. Industrialization can occur anywhere. The social theories developed in the West do not necessarily explain what is happening in Japan. The same level of industrialization does not imply an identical social structure in different cultures. According to Chie Nakane, the Japanese society is vertically structured. Human relations between society and different groups, as well as relations between different groups, remain basically the same when society and culture change (Nakane 1970; Nakane 1991; Gluck 1978, 25-50).[4]

There are still characteristics of old kinship relations in the social system, working life and family life of the Japanese society. Kizaemoni Ariga in his book from the year 1943 depicts the rural social system. In the rural economy, the relation between the landlord and his peasants has been like a family relationship rather than a feudal one. People have lived in extended family relationships, which Ariga considers a special Japanese characteristic. The independence of peasants meant a system of rent payment. Rent was not a labour rent, but a product rent. It was paid according to the product, not labour (Kawamura 1988, 275; Ariga 1969).

Ariga stresses the nature of the kinship model with vertical and hierarchical relations. Horizontal social relations in this male hierarchy have only been provisional, *kumi* relations, which have tended to be equal relations. The basis has been in the vertical and hierarchical structure. The horizontal relations have always been typically female, and nowadays the community relations, too, are horizontal and female in nature.

When trying to analyse the modern Japaneses business firms, researchers have used the extended family relationships to describe the social hierarchy of the firm. In the urban economy, just like in the rural one, the whole socio-economic hierarchical structure has been based on men. Women have been in a subordinate category.

The Japanese emphasize the uniqueness of their society, but at the same time they borrow phenomena from the West and mix these elements into their own culture. In the meantime they preserve the core of their own culture untouched. This core gives energy to the whole culture and allows it to assimilate strange superficial phenomena into the Japanese culture, Nakane stresses. She maintains that it is easier to import civilisation and technology than spirit and culture.

The Japanese culture is considered highly ritualistic. People in a way ritualize new imported phenomena by Japanizing everything. Ritualization is done by means of rules. There are rules for everything, and everything happens like in a game. With the help of the game the Japanese are able to make anything into something practical. Rituals are not informative, because they are self-evidences. Consequently, it is understandable that the Japanese are not worried about the Americanization of their everyday life, although outsiders often see it as a threat. Japanese people have made their own rules concerning this phenomenon and understand that as long as they use their own cultural rules, they are in control of the situation. That is why the new phenomena, imported from the West, do not threaten them.

Some Western theories stress the total nature of culture. In other words, you cannot take some parts, like technology, for example, from one culture and transfer it to another. The spiritual and material issues are inseparable. Some anthropologists have warned us against the Americanization of the whole world.[5] As examples they have given the transfer of technology from the industrialized countries to the Third World, as well as the American cultural invasion with its language and habits. The postmodern cultural characteristics of another wave of this invasion are represented by the McDonaldization or Disneylandization of the world in the 1990s. As institutions, both are well-known and alive in Japan, too. In Nakane's opinion, however, the Japanese culture is old and strong. It is able to keep its social system unchanged, relying on its own basic principles.

In the 1980s, the Japanese economy became one of the strongest in the world. Consequently, impacts started flowing in the opposite direction, too, from the East to the West. In addition to being economically powerful, Japan wanted to be strong culturally.

According to Nozomu Kawamura, the Japanese society may in the future take the form of a new communal society (Kawamura 1988, 278-281), transforming from modern society to postmodern. In Japan this means that some elements of the preindustrial community will be revived with the establishment of the new group formation. Two factors will help the process of revival: the right wing conservative element and the left wing progressive one. Japan is the only capitalistic society which has achieved a high level of development without sharing the cultural tradition of Western Europe. It has combined the feudal and Asiatic elements. Large corporations and monopoly capitalists can make positive use of the remnants of communal relations. These relations facilitate the

118

formation of a new communal society. If economic motives demand it, women, too, will be real members of this new economically formulated communal society. The ideas of women's liberation imported from the West are not the cause of this development. Instead, the Japanese society is adapting itself for reasons of survival, not because of Western ideology.

Nakane discusses the impact of the Western culture on the Japanese society and points out that the Japanese social system will change slowly (Nakane 1990, 303-306). The Japanese system will change only when reasons of survival and development demand it. In other words, social policy systems and services will be expanded and developed, if the new position of women becomes necessary and if a more developed social policy is needed for the success of society and for a more effective use of the female labour (Tsurumi 1988).

In the last few decades, the middle class values have supported the economic miracle of Japan. The model of the housewife has been in the focus of this development. Housewives have helped their husbands in their demanding duties, they have looked after the children and have also helped financially so that the children have been able to go to school and evening classes. Housewives have also paid for their children's hobbies. In addition, they have cared for not only their own parents but also their parents-in-law. As part-time employees, too, the wives have had the identity of housewives. The housewife has been like a magical being, because she has had a social function in society, not a direct material function. She has been the soul of society. With the housewife institution, the economy has changed. One reality has changed into another (Trabant 1989, 126-130).

Behind this ideal model, however, there has been a great variety of lifestyles. If the husband has been a blue-collar worker, for example, the wife may have worked temporarily, but still all her life, either at home for some factory or in a small business outside the home. The majority of firms in Japan are very small, which means that the whole family, frequently an extended family, are working for the firm: the wife, the grandparents, the sons and daughters, and other relatives. The myth of the housewife as an ideal in the Japanese society has in many circles been literally a myth. Masculine spirit and hegemony have focused on the big firms, and it is in these circles that the women's invasion of new hierarchical levels is a novelty.

When women with children have worked in small businesses, they have in most cases taken care of their children themselves. When the women have transferred into a more visible world and have become permanent workers in big enterprises, new arrangements have been necessary: the new situation demands social services. In Finland the majority of women have for decades worked outside their homes, and they have traditionally worked on a permanent basis, not temporarily or as part-time employees. The demands of the female workforce made the development of a major social policy system necessary, since urbanization, occurring at the same time, resulted in the formation of core or nuclear families. The relatives of young mothers often live far away, and for a long time most families have had to manage without daily help from relatives. This has caused the need for public social services. At the same time the educational level of women has risen, and the educated women have been able to demand better services. The educational level of women in Finland is higher on average than that of men.[6] Against this background it is interesting for an outsider to speculate on how the process of making women more visible in Japan will succeed.

The problem of intertextuality in handling different texts runs the risk of the subject dying in the different phases of interpretation. The text has been constructed by a mosaic of citations. The reader of the text as the recipient construes it and gives it meanings (Eco 1981). In this context, results of empirical research conducted in Japan or outside it have been used. The picture of the Japanese women is based on different narratives of women, and of their conditions and position in society. The present narrative provides one perspective, and one interpretation or understanding, of the Japanese women in their society. The position of women in society is an element which perhaps the most critically distinguishes Finland from Japan. In many other characteristics these two societies are remarkably similar.

For a very long time, the Japanese woman has been magically and ritualistically understood as the young geisha, the *maiko* girl, with her heavy white mask which hides all her woman's feelings and presents her as an obedient servant. This woman has the role of an understanding mother, as well as that of a muse for her tired husband (Fraser & Nicholson 1988; Allen & Young 1989). The muse has now begun to ponder new ideas which are leading her into the world of men, until now kept secret from her. In reality, though, the Japanese women have been active members of their society all along. It is only their position in the public life that has been more hidden than the position of men.

Feminist theories in the West are changing all the time. Some recent trends focus on crosscultural or transepochal interpretation in which the mode of attention is comparative rather than universal. Such an approach is more interested in changes and contrasts than general laws. Such a theory replaces unitary notions with plural and complex conceptions of social identity, treating gender as one relevant factor among many others. It recognizes the diversity of women's needs and experiences. No single way of life can be adequate for all. Interests are by no means universal, they are even in conflict with each other. (Miyoshi & Harootunian 1989, 390-391.)

Reality of life of the Japanese women fits this theoretical approach. In a way, for historical reasons the Japanese women are in 'the same boat', but at the same time their living conditions differ considerably. The gap between two groups of women is growing: the forerunners are breaking their way into the masculine world, while some other women continue to live in a more traditional feminine way.

Notes

1. According to a study made by Nozawa & Takahashi (1990) in Tokyo, self-employed men whose place of residence is vitally important for their business, as well as non-employed men, show a strong commitment to their local community. Blue-collar workers form work place centred networks, while white-collar workers establish the widest personal networks spatially and according to the social context of the network.

2. The old household institution, ie, with its ancestor worship and inheritance rules, has been regarded and propagated as a necessary basis for the modern society. The ie-system was coded in legal terms in the Meiji Civil Code, finally promulgated in 1898. Ancestor worship and filial piety together with emperor worship and loyalty were legally codified towards the end of

the Second World War, replacing the old Civil Code which had been rooted in the traditional, patriarchal structure of household, with legal consequences to family status, inheritance, continuation of the house and ancestor worship. Revision included modern democratic principles, such as respect for the individual, equality of the sexes and freedom of belief. It provided respect for different family structures. The household is no more a legal entity and its head is stripped of his power. Legally Japan turned away from the old ie-structure and moved in the direction of the Western nuclear family model.

The New Civil Code was finally enforced in 1948 after which ancestor worship has been a custom rather than a legal obligation. As a result of urbanization and growth of nuclear families, many families are free from parish ties and the old ie-system. More than 70 per cent of the population live in nuclear families (Linhart, S. 1976).

3. Yoshiwara has been one of the most famous pleasure quarters in Tokyo in the Tokugawa and the Meiji period (Longstreet & Longstreet 1988).

4. One explanation of the unique character of Japanese experience of nature. Japan's mild climate is rich in variation. For example, Watsuji Tetsuro, one of Japan's profoundest theorists focuses on the uniquely Japanese awareness of the passing seasons (Watsuji 1971).

5. One of them is a Finnish anthropologist Matti Sarmela, who speaks about cultural imperialism (Sarmela 1989).

6. Even if the educational level of women in Finland is high, the average wage level of women compared with that of men is still lower and has not changed proportionally: wage level of women/men 79.5 per cent in 1985, 80.0 per cent in 1986, 1987 and 1988, 79.7 per cent in 1989 and 79.5 per cent in 1990. (Katsaus 1990, 47).

References

Allen, Jeffner & Young, Iris Marion (eds.) (1989), *The Thinking Muse. Feminism and Modern French Philosophy*, Indiana University Press, Bloomington and Indianapolis.

Ariga, Kizaemon chosakushu (The Collected Works of Ariga

Kizaemon) (1969), Vol VIII, Tokyo.

Berentsen, Jan-Martin (1985), *Grave and Gospel*, E.J. Brill, Leiden.

Bestor, Theodore C. (1989), *Neighborhood Tokyo*, Stanford University Press, Stanford, California.

Eco, Umberto (1981), *The Role of the Reader. Explorations in the Semiotics of Texts*, Hutchinson, London.

Family and Community in Japan (1986), National Report of the Japanese National Committee, ICSW, Tokyo.

Fornander, Kjell (1990), *La Dolce Vita of Office Ladies*, Scanorama, September.

Fraser, Nancy & Nicholson, Linda (1988), 'Social Criticism without Philosophy: An Encounter between Feminism and Post-modernism', *Theory, Culture & Society*, Vol. 5, Number 2-3, June.

Gluck, Carol (1978), 'The People in History: Recent Trends in Japanese Historiography', *Journal of Asian Studies*, Vol. XXXVIII, No. 1, November.

Imamura, Anne E. (1988), *A Window on Her World: The Relevance of Housing Type for the Urban Japanese Housewife*, Van Vliet, Villem (ed.), Women, Housing and Community, Avebury.

Japan Labor Bulletin (1994), Vol. 33 - No. 9.

Japan Labor Bulletin (1994), Vol. 33 - No. 10.

Japanese Working Life Profile 1988 (1988), The Japan Institute of Labour, Tokyo.

Japanese Working Life Profile 1993-94 (1992), The Japan Institute of Labour, Tokyo.

Kato, Shuichi (1988), *A History of Japanese Literature. The Modern Years*, Volume 3, Hong Kong.

Katsaus (1990), *Tilastollinen aikakauslehti* 4.

Kawamura, Nozomu (1988), *The Concept of Modernization Re-examined*, in the book of McCormack & Sugimoto.

Linhart, Ruth (1986), 'Frauen treten aus dem Schatten — die Japanerinnen 1945-1985', in Linhart, Sepp (Hrsg.), *40 Jahre modernes Japan, Schriftenreihe Japankunde*, Wien.

Linhart, Sepp (1976), *Arbeit, Freizeit und Familie in Japan*, Schriften des Instituts für Asienkunde in Hamburg, Band 43, Wiesbaden.

Longstreet, Stephen & Longstreet, Ethel (1988), *Yoshiwara. The Pleasure Quarters of Old Tokyo*, C.E. Tuttle Co., Tokyo.

McCormack, Gavan & Sugimoto, Yoshio (eds.) (1988), *The Japanese Trajectory: Modernization and Beyond*, Cambridge University Press,

Cambridge.

Miyoshi, Masao & Harootunian, H.D. (eds.) (1989), *Postmodernism in Japan*, Duke University Press, Durham (NC) and London.

Nakane, Chie (1970), *Japanese Society*, Weidenfeld & Nicholson, London.

Nakane, Chie (1991), Japanese Society: Continuity and Change, and Japanese Society: Its Distinguishing Features, in Koskiaho, Briitta et al. (eds.), *The Essence of Japanese Society. Nordic and Japanese Interpretations*, Acta Universitatis Tamperensis, Ser B vol 35, Tampere.

Nakane, Chie (1990), Interview, in article: Koskiaho, Briitta, *Japani japanilaisten tulkitsemana*, Kanava 5.

Nozawa, Shinji & Takahashi, Yuetsu (1990), *Subcultural Differentiation of Inner Tokyo, Personal Networks and Local Community*, Summarized English Versions of Recent Publications of Sogo Toshi Kenkyu, No. 39, March 1990, Tokyo Metropolitan University, Center for Urban Studies, Tokyo.

Pateman, Carole (1988), *Sexual Contract*, Stanford University Press, Stanford, California.

Refsing, Kirsten et al. (1990), *Gode hustruer og vise mødre*, The University of Copenhagen, Copenhagen.

Sarmela, Matti (1989), *Rakennemuutos tulevaisuuteen, Postlokaalinen maailma ja Suomi*, WSOY, Juva.

Saxonhouse, Gary R. (1976), 'Country Girls and Communication among Competitors in the Japanese Cotton-Spinning Industry', in Patrick, Hugh (ed.), *Japanese Industrialization and Its Social Consequences*, University of California Press, Berkeley and Los Angeles.

Slawik, Alexander & Linhart, Sepp (Hrsg.) (1981), *Die Japanerinnen in Vergangenheit und Gegenwart*, Referate des 2, Wiener Japanologengesprächs vom 9. bis 11. April 1980, Beiträge zur Japanologie, Band 17, Wien.

Solo, Sally (1989), *Japan Discovers Woman Power*, Fortune, June 19.

Teichler, Ulrich (1973), 'Der japanische Bildungsreformplan', in Wittig, Horst G. (Hrsg.), *Menschenbildung in Japan*, München.

Trabant, Jürgen (1989), *Zeichen des Menschen. Elemente der Semiotik*, Fischer Taschenbuch Verlag, Frankfurt am Main.

Tsurumi, E. Patricia (ed.) (1988), *The Other Japan. Postwar Realities*, M.E. Sharpe, Armonk & New York & London.

Watsuji, Tetsuro (1971), *Climate and Culture*, Hokuseido, Tokyo.

Women of Japan: Conditions and Policies (without year), Report on the National Plan of Action (2), Prime Minister's Office, Tokyo.

Women Workers in Japan (1988), National Institute of Employment and Vocational Research, NIEV Report No. 4, March, Tokyo.

Women's Occupation Careers in Japan (1988), National Institute of Employment and Vocational Research, NIEV Report, No. 4, March, Tokyo.

Working Women in Japan (1989), Women's Bureau, Ministry of Labour, Japan Institute of Women's Employment, Tokyo.

Appendix

Table 1
Time spent per weekday on activities by sex and economic activity
(average for all persons)

in hours.minutes

Sex	Sleep	Personal care	Meals	Commuting to and from school or work	Work	School work	House keeping	Nursing and child care	Shop-ping	Leisure activities
Males and females	7.25	1.02	1.32	0.52	7.25	0.05	1.01	0.07	0.13	3.38
Working men	7.34	0.53	1.30	1.00	8.17	0.05	0.05	0.03	0.05	3.48
Working women	7.14	1.14	1.34	0.41	6.12	0.05	2.19	0.15	0.25	3.23
Women not working	7.42	1.15	1.46	0.15	0.06	1.12	3.29	0.43	0.36	5.35

Working persons are defined as 'those who usually work to earn income', including 'those mainly working', 'those working while keeping house' and 'those working while attending school'.

Source: Statistical Bureau, Management and Coordination Agency, 1991 Survey on time use and leisure activities, Volume 6. Japan Labor Bulletin, October 1, 1994.

Table 2
Factors that deter women from continuing to work

Child care	61.4 %
Medical care for the elderly	45.3 %
Household chores	27.7 %
Children's education	27.2 %
Insufficient working environment	26.9 %
Own health	24.2 %
Lack of family member's understanding	24.0 %
Transfer of husband's workplace	19.7 %
Retirement system based on marriage or childbirth	12.5 %
Biased notion toward women's ability and motivation	12.3 %
Inequality in promotion and training	7.9 %

Source: Prime Minister's Office, Public Opinion Poll on Women's Work (1989). Japan Labor Bulletin, October 1, 1994.

6 The changing women's employment and the role of social policies in Japan

Machiko Osawa

The purpose of this paper is to discuss the effect of the Japanese social policies on the women's decision to work. The paper focuses on the social security system, taxation and family policies in the context of a changing family structure and employment opportunities.

The overall picture of working Japanese women is as follows. Due to the service economy and new technology, a larger number of educated women are entering the labour market. However, women's tenure (continuous service) is still short compared with the other countries, and women tend not to continue working after they marry and have children.

Until recently, this pattern of women's work and their exclusion from the labour force did not worry the Japanese. However, due to the decline in the birth rate in the 1970s, the shortage of youth labour was a constraint on the economic growth of Japan, so that employment of women as workers became necessary.

In addition, the declining fertility among recent young cohorts generated concerns about a labour shortage and a rapid ageing of the Japanese society. Due to the delay of marriage among young cohorts, the fertility rate sank to a record low 1.40 in 1993. If the birth rate continues to decline, the burden of supporting the old generation will grow heavier and the number of workers supporting one retired person will decrease from an estimated 7 to a little over 3 between 1990 and 2020. It was in this context of a growing shortage of labour and the problem of the elderly that the public started to pay more attention to the issue of working women

127

and the difficulties they have in trying to both work and raise children.

The relatively weak employment attachment of well-educated women is related to social policy (i.e. social security and the taxation system) in Japan.

Taxation and the social security system

Income tax

In principle, taxes are levied on individuals. It is in sharp contrast to the U.K., the U.S. and France where the tax unit is the family. Accordingly, married couples in Japan with the same total income pay different taxes, depending on whether there are two wage-earners or one.

However, a deduction can be made from the husband's taxable income (350,000 yen), if the wife earns less than 1.2 million yen a year as an income and if the living costs are paid by the head of the household (husband). Women earning below this amount are not subject to income tax. (This figure is based on the fiscal year of 1991.)

This income ceiling for dependents in households has been rising since it was introduced in 1961, but it is still rather low. Exemption from taxes at a relatively low level of income has served to discourage full-time work and is based on the assumption that women serve as unpaid corporate workers, allowing men to concentrate on their careers. The consequence of this policy has been that married women are employed in poorly paid part-time jobs in which they receive no benefits or bonuses. Corporations benefit from this pool of labour because increased reliance on part-time workers enables corporations to compensate for and subsidize the rigidities of prevailing employment practices for core employees. In some firms, company housing benefits are linked to the wife's income, creating an additional disincentive to work full time, given the staggering cost of housing in Japan.

The problem of this taxation system is not only that it creates a disincentive for wives to work full time (or earn more than the income ceiling), but it is also regressive in that the ceiling applies across-the-board regardless of the husband's income. Thus families from vastly different tax brackets find that they are lumped together when it comes to the income ceiling of the dependents.

Social security system

The Japanese social security system for households whose head is a paid employee is a two-tier system. First there is the basic pension. Regardless of contribution, everyone receives a minimum amount each month. The second part of the pension reflects the employees' contributions. This is called *Kosei-rôrei-nenkin*.

Everyone who is working is obliged to pay a social security payment. This is about 14.5 per cent of earned income. Actually the rate is different for men and women. The rate for women, however, has been rising gradually and was equal by 1994. This cost is split between employers and employees, but it does not concern individuals classified as dependent on the head of the household.

For a variety of reasons, women who work less make out better under the existing social security scheme. Women who earn less than 1.2 million do not have to pay social security tax but receive the basic benefit that everybody gets. In addition, because they are defined as dependents, they also receive a dependent's allowance. Thus, the tax and pension system reinforce women's roles by financial inducements and penalties that make part-time work more attractive. This also serves as a disincentive for those who choose careers.

This also raises the issue of inequality of burden between single-earner (or one and half earner with wife's income less than 1.2 million) and two-earner households in which the wife earns more than 1.2 million yen.

The second problem of this system is that a working wife whose husband dies has to choose either her own pension (*kosei-rôrei-nenkin*) or her husband's pension. Usually a woman stops working to raise her children or to take care of her elderly parents so that her own pension is less than her husband's *izoku-nenkin* (widow benefit). Consequently, she is more likely to choose her husband's pension. As a result, she loses her own benefit despite her contributions. Thus working women are penalized since they must give up their own earned pension benefits if they choose their widow benefits. This means that they and women who never worked can receive similar pensions, creating another disincentive to work.

Health insurance

Those who reside in Japan are covered by either the national or a company health insurance system. The company insurance covers 90 per cent of the medical costs of employees. If you are a dependent of an employee, 70 per cent of the medical costs are covered and no premium is charged.

Employment insurance

The employment insurance provides income when an individual falls ill or is disabled during work. It also provides income for the unemployed. The contributions to the employment insurance, paid by employers, differ by industry. Employers must pay this insurance for all their regular workers and part-timers who fulfil the conditions stipulated below:
1. The number of working hours is from 22 to 33 hours per week.
2. The annual income is over 900,000 yen.
3. The work contract is for more than a year.

Employers do not have to pay employment insurance, if part-timers work less than 22 hours per week. This encourages employers to hire part-timers, if full-timers and part-timers are equally productive.

Benefits of a full-time housewife in Japan

From the above discussion, it is clear that Japanese social policies, such as the system of taxation and social security, are based on traditional single-earner households. Consequently, social policy has failed to keep pace with the changing economic structure and the Japanese economy is compelled to draw on the human resources of women. The existing system is replete with disincentives which discourage and prevent women from pursuing careers. In this section, I shall discuss the overall benefits of Japanese housewives (including those who work but earn less than the taxable amount).

The benefits of a dependent housewife include: (1) reduction in income tax, (2) exemption from paying social security contribution, (3) free health insurance, and (4) family allowance included in the

130

husband's earnings.

Family allowances are based on the idea that the family's need for support should determine the salary. The amount is larger, the larger the firm. In 1988, large firms paid 14,000 yen a month on average for the family allowance, the medium size firms 8,700 yen and small size firms 6,300 yen.

According to Kimura (1990), these benefits amount to 424,000 yen per year on average if the wife is 38 years of age and the husband works for a large company and his annual income is 8 million yen. On the other hand, if the husband works for a small size firm and his annual income is 5 million yen, this benefit amounts to 304,000 yen. Consequently, the benefit of being a housewife is greater in the higher income brackets.

It has been pointed out that wage differentials related to the size of the firm are quite large in Japan and are considered a distinctive characteristic of the Japanese labour market. In fact, wage differentials widened during the 1980s.

Paradoxically, women who are highly educated are less likely to be working. This is because most probably they are married to husbands who are also well educated and employed at a large corporation. As a result, the Japanese system provides disincentives to work for women with high human capital accumulation and educational attainment. This is one of the reasons why the situation in Japan is so different from that of the other OECD countries. Highly educated women do not have a strong attachment to the labour force and the correlation between schooling and participation in the labour force is virtually absent.

The changing family structure and family policy

The transformation of the Japanese society during the so-called economic miracle and beyond has been extraordinary. However, these changes have not been accompanied by commensurate changes in social policy. Women's patterns of work, resulting from these economic changes, continue despite inappropriate public policies. Although the Japanese social security system seems to discourage careers for women, there is a need for more women workers. Consequently, women's wages are increasing and women's tenure (continuous service) has lengthened accordingly.

In 1960, the average length of tenure was 4 years, rising to 7.4 years in 1991. In addition, more and more married women participate in the labour force so that in 1992 the number of two-earner households surpassed that of single-earner households.

One of the significant changes affecting families is the rising divorce rate. Between 1970 and 1988 there was a 30.5 per cent drop in the number of marriages and a 54.8 per cent rise in the number of divorces. It is illustrative that the number of divorces registered in 1970 equalled to 9.3 per cent of registered marriages for that year, while in 1988 the number of divorces equalled to 58.4 per cent of the number of marriages. The number of divorces rose steadily from 95,937 in 1970 to 179,191 in 1992. The divorce rate rose from 0.93 per thousand in 1970 to 1.45 per thousand in 1992.

There are two distinctive peaks in the divorce rate, namely among young couples married less than five years and among older couples married over twenty years. The rise in the overall divorce rate can be attributed, among other things, to women's greater economic independence. Today they are not forced to endure an unhappy marriage because of economic dependence. In addition, social mores have been changing and the same kind of stigma is no longer attached to divorce as in the past. Traditional constraints, which previously depressed the divorce rates, do not seem to restrict today's young couples.

Among older couples, divorce is rising as a result of undeveloped relationships when the couple cannot cope with the strain of the husband's retirement. It is quite stunning to note that from 1970 to 1985, divorce as the reason for ending a marriage of 18 or 19 years rose from 19.1 per cent to 49.3 per cent. Given the priority of work and the common practice of gender segregated socializing, couples have a difficult time in developing communication and shared interests. When suddenly faced with the husband's retirement, a growing number of women have opted for divorce. With no children to worry about any more, and given the longer life expectancy, more and more women choose not to endure an elongated post-retirement life in an unhappy marriage. It is quite telling that a new expression, *sodai gomi* (a large piece of garbage) is now used to refer to retired husbands and their propensity to get in the way around the house.

As a result of rising divorce rates, the number of single parent households is increasing. From 1970 to 1986, the proportion of

132

single parent households of total households increased from 2.9 per cent to 4.1 per cent. Their average income per capita is only 38.7 per cent of average household income in 1988.

According to a survey conducted by the Ministry of Labour, women say that child care and the care of the elderly are the two biggest obstacles which prevent them from working.

Day care

The Japanese public day care system appears to be quite well established and of high quality. Despite its good reputation, however, the system is only made use of to a limited degree. It is quite inflexible and involves a number of restrictions which do not take into account women's work and commuting schedules.

Table 1 shows who looks after children while the mother is working. When a child is less than one year old, 67.2 per cent of full-time working mothers depend on their own mother to look after the child. This proportion is gradually declining and there is a growing number of those who use private or public day care centres. The public day care fee depends on household income. The higher the household income, the higher the fee. Due to the decline in the fertility rate, getting a place in the public day care centre is not too difficult, but the hours often make it difficult for women in full-time jobs to take advantage of this system. Fees for private day care average about 67,000 yen a month as of 1988.

Table 1
Care of children while mother is working, per cent

	Age of youngest child	
	< 1	1 ≤ 7
Work only when child already in kindergarten	-	15.0
Husband	4.2	3.6
Grandparents	67.2	51.0
Baby-sitter	1.5	1.0
Neighbours or friend of the family	2.7	2.1
Day care centre (both public & private)	28.9	49.8
Other	1.2	1.2

Source: Fujin shonen Kyoku, Report on Working Mother, 1989

133

One of the problems of the Japanese public day care system is that few places accept children under one year age. The other problem is the restrictive hours. Most full-time women work after 5 p.m., so that many have to find another place for their child in addition to the public day care. This means significant additional costs and logistical problems.

Even if a public day care centre is available, many working women rely on their own or their husband's mother because of longer working hours in Japan. While many firms have adapted to a 5-day work schedule, they have simultaneously increased the daily working hours. This has made it even harder for mothers to work. Consequently, living in an extended household increases the women's probability to work as full-time employees by about 17 per cent (Osawa 1993).

The increase in the number of working mothers, and perhaps the decline in the fertility rate as well, induced the government to enact Child Care Leave. The Child Care Leave bill was approved by the Diet in 1991. The purpose of the law is to provide a better environment for both men and women to participate in paid work as well as in child raising. Under this law, workers in the private sector are allowed to take leaves of absence until their child is one year old. There is no compensation during the leave, but jobs are guaranteed.

The outline of the new legislation is as follows (Japan Labor Bulletin, July, 1991).

1. Employees of both sexes can take child care leave up until the child turns one by clarifying the period of the leave.

2. Companies are forbidden to fire employees for taking leave.

3. Companies should in advance stipulate the treatment of their employees on child care leave, as well as their wages and positions after the end of the leave. Also, they should endeavour to take the necessary steps and ensure flexibility for employees who take the leave and return to work after the leave.

4. Companies should take measures, such as shortening the hours of work, for those employees who care for a child under the age of one and who do not take the leave. Furthermore, they should make efforts to institutionalize the child care leave or the shortening of the hours of work, including workers who care for

134

a child over the age of one.

5. The government should give advice, guidance and recommendations to companies for an effective implementation of the Child Care Leave Law.

6. Companies with a work-force of 30 employees or less will be given a three years' grace period to implement the law.

This law became effective on April 1, 1992.

The major issue regarding this law was whether it would guarantee an income during the leave. So far it has not done it, drawing criticism since many workers cannot afford a leave without pay. In addition, there are no enforcement powers so it is more like a guideline.

In 1990, prior to the enactment of the 1992 Child Care Leave Act, 21.9 per cent of firms with over thirty employees reported having a child care leave system in place. In 1992, following the enactment of the law, 50.8 per cent of firms with over thirty employees reported that they complied with its provisions. According to a survey conducted in July 1992, 90 per cent of the labour unions reported having negotiated arrangements for a child care leave system. Union surveys suggest that in order for women to cope with the burden of child rearing, it is necessary to introduce flex-time or shorter working hours after the initial year of leave.

Care of elderly parents

Another major problem facing working mothers is the care of elderly parents. At this moment, there is no law to allow women or men to take leave for caring for their parents, nor is there any special assistance from the government. As of 1989, only 17 per cent of firms allow their employees to take a leave to care for their elderly parents. However, if the parents are dependent and older than 60, a certain amount of money can be deducted from the taxable income of the head of the household regardless of the costs of care.

Women are expected to take primary responsibility for the care of their ageing parents and parents-in-law. The system of the care of the elderly remains relatively undeveloped and until recently the government has based its planning and policies on the assumption

135

that the elderly are cared for by their families, i.e. women relatives. One of the problems is that the three-generation family is declining in Japan, accounting for only 13.1 per cent of all families. Of households with at least one member over the age of 65, 35.9 per cent are extended families.

Belatedly, the government has unveiled plans to improve facilities and services for the elderly. This will take some time, however, and it will be difficult to keep pace with the rapidly rising numbers of elderly in need of such services. It is more and more obvious that policy makers have been too optimistic about the capacity of families to cope with the care of the elderly in the absence of significant public support. Recent surveys suggest that families have expressed less than enthusiastic support for taking care of their elderly parents, while women have been most averse to such arrangements. In a recent government survey only 23 per cent of the respondents indicated that they would take care of their parents at any cost, compared to 63 per cent in the U.S. The Asahi newspaper conducted a similar survey in 1994, finding that 68 per cent of women in their late 1930s and 1940s did not want to take care of their parents, while 60 per cent of women in their 1950s gave a similar response.

In light of the fact that the Japanese population is ageing more rapidly than the population of any other industrialized nation, an estimated 25 per cent of the population will be over age 65 by the year 2018. Consequently, the inadequacy of government programmes will weigh heavily on women well into the 21st century. Looking to the future, women's participation in the active work force may decline because of the demands of caring for their aged relatives. This prospect could have a detrimental impact on the economy, worsening an impending labour shortage, denying corporate Japan the various advantages associated with the employment of women workers, and lessening government tax revenues precisely at a time when the outlay for an ageing society will rise dramatically. Thus, for a variety of reasons, it is crucial that public services and facilities for the aged be developed to better assist women in reconciling the demands of work and family.

The Equal Employment Opportunity Law (EEOL), enacted in 1986, was designed to eliminate discrimination in corporate employment practices. This law has come under fire because of the absence of enforcement measures and the doubts about the efficacy of relying on voluntary compliance. However, it does seem that corporate Japan has upheld the letter, if not the spirit, of the EEOL. There have been a variety of administrative changes in hiring and employment practices that appear to be more favourable to women employees. For example, firms now offer qualified women the choice of employment in the managerial track which involves intensive training and job rotation throughout the firm, as well as enhanced prospects for career development. There is considerable debate over whether it is due to women's own disinclination, their continued discrimination or a system tailored to male employees, but it is clear that women are not taking advantage of this system in great numbers. In general, the EEOL seems to have had little impact on the prevailing patriarchal employment practices in Japan during the 1980s and women's return on education remains lower than men's despite the fact that more women are studying what have traditionally been considered male, job-oriented disciplines. Women still act as shock absorbers for the relatively rigid employment system created for the mostly male, core labour force.

Participation in the active work force among women has been rising most rapidly in part-time jobs with the attendant disadvantages in terms of job security, benefits and salaries. In the summer of 1994 there was a media furore over the widely reported refusal of firms to even grant interviews to recently graduated female job candidates, much less make job offers. It appears that when times get tough as they have during the longest postwar recession in the 1990s, women are still treated as if they are expendable, EEOL or not. This suggests that the lack of an enforcement mechanism will continue to vitiate the potential of this legislation for advancing women workers' interests and status in the economy.

Conclusion

It is quite clear from the above discussion that Japanese social policies are based upon the traditional households, such as a single-earner household or two-earners if the wife provides supplemental income to the household. In the process of economic change, however, the number of traditional households has declined and two-earners, single parents and single households are increasing so that the role of the family as the fulcrum of social security has been weakened tremendously. There is an urgent need to craft new social policies better suited to current realities. Without enlightened government policies it will be difficult to cope with the strains of the changes and to ensure future prosperity. It is necessary to lessen the obstacles to women's careers so that the nation can gain from their contribution more fully.

References

En, Fukki (1992), 'Women's Labor Force Participation and Educational Attainment: U.S. Japan and China Comparison', *Keizaigaku Kenkyu*, University of Hiroshima, March.

Ishi, Hiromitsu (1989), *The Japanese Taxation System*, Oxford: Oxford University Press.

The Japan Institute of Labor (1991), *Japan Labor Bulletin*, July.

Kimura, Yoko (1990), 'Taxation for Housewife and Social Security System', Institute for the Social Security, Discussion Paper.

Miyajima, Hiroshi (1992), *Socio-Economics in the Aging Society*, Iwanamishoten, Tokyo.

Osawa, Machiko (1993), *Economic Change and Women Workers: U.S. and Japan Comparison*, Nihon Keizai Hyoronsha.

7 The level of living and social security of the elderly in Japan

Sachiko Matsumura

Viewpoint of analysis

In the past the elderly in Japan were quite dependent on their children in terms of their financial affairs and their nursing care. This was due to the high rate of sharing a house. However, now they tend to live separately and independently of their children. 'Basic Survey of National Living' (1989) by the Ministry of Health and Welfare shows that 42 per cent share their house with a married child and 18 per cent share it with a single child, while 26 per cent are living with their spouse, 1 per cent are single, and 3 per cent are others among the total of 14,239,000 over 65-year-old Japanese people.

As the living independence of the elderly progresses, the structure of their living expenditure is changing. Compared with the expenditure of other generations, their living expenditure includes a high pension cost in their income and high food expenses, medical payments, and entertainment allowance. As they begin separating from their children, this feature is highlighted. For example, the income proportion of an aged household (a household composed of only a man over 65 years and a woman over 60 years, or a household composed of these elderly and children under 18 years) consists of 50 per cent in pensions, 34 per cent in salaries, 10 per cent in income from properties, and 3 per cent in social insurance except pensions (welfare, a disability benefit from various insurances, a compensation for business suspension and so on), 3 per cent in other incomes.

Calculating from the number of households, the rate of households whose 'income is 100 per cent from pension' is increasing year by year, and had already reached 49 per cent in 1988. On the other hand, the fact that the wage and salary income is over 30 per cent is a characteristic of the Japanese. Compared with other advanced countries, the employment rate of the elderly in our country is high. The employment income accounts for an important part of the living expenditure of the elderly.

Households with an aged couple

There is a difference in the conditions in that an elderly couple's rate of home ownership is much higher than that of young couples (Table 1). However, the monthly living expenditure of households of an elderly couple with an earner is similar to that of young couples. Figure 1 shows the distribution of living expenditure of these 3 types of households. Households consisting of an elderly couple have a higher rate of food expenditure and a high proportion of other expenditures (such as allowances for entertainment) than households of young couples. Households of young couples, in turn, have twice as much housing expenditure and transportation and communication expenditure. Especially, households of an aged couple without an earner have a high proportion of food expenditure at 27 per cent, and their housing expenditure proportion is higher than that of households of an aged couple with an earner. These facts help us see how insufficient their living conditions are.

Provision conditions for public pension

When asked in the survey of National Living about 'a viewpoint on the present financial conditions', households with a 60 year-old and older head replied 'living without any worry' (15 per cent), 'living without any serious worry' (61 per cent), 'anxious without leeway' (17 per cent), and 'living in very severe conditions' (3 per cent).

140

Table 1
Households with an aged couple (all households)

	Households with an aged couple with earner	Households with an aged couple without earner	Households with a young couple
Earners per household	1.30	-	1.49
Age of household head	70.0	72.0	26.5
Rate of owned houses (%)	91.0	84.1	15.8
Yearly income (thousand yen)	5,566	3,118	4,530
Living expenditure per month (yen)	236,432	198,676	235,737

Source: 1989 National Survey of Family Income and Expenditure, Statistics Bureau, Management and Coordination Agency, Japan.

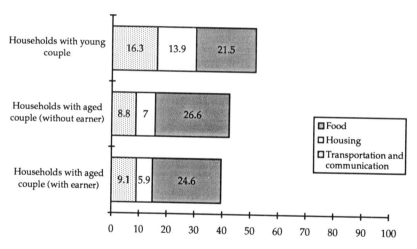

Figure 1 Percentage distribution of living expenditure (food, housing and transportation & communication) per month by items of households with an aged couple (all households)

Source: 1989 National Survey of Family Income and Expenditure. Statistics Bureau, Management and Coordination Agency, Japan.

141

Compared with the situation five years ago, people who replied 'living in very severe conditions' have decreased. However, people with 'anxiety without leeway' are increasing. With the rapid progress of the ageing society, there seems to be many people with a worry or two. Moreover, when asked about 'necessities for the elderly to live comfortably', they pointed to an expansion of the public pension system (73 per cent) as their first choice, an expansion of the medical treatment system for the elderly (58 per cent) as their second choice, and the stability of prices (including land and house prices) as their third.

The present elderly, who survived the chaotic period during and after the Second World War and who worked to support the high economic growth following the war, appreciate the increase of the present material level which is high compared with the other periods of their life. However, they are confused with the change at home and the reduction of space which could not have been conceived in earlier times and cry over the diminished human relationships. These appear in 'expansion for public and private nursing facility services for the elderly' (35 per cent) and 'securing a place for mutual discussion for people in the area' (16 per cent) of the same research.

Elderly life in Japan is changing drastically. Food and clothing have become abundant and leisure has increased. The elderly do not clearly know 'what kind of life-style for the elderly is appropriate in this new period'. It seems to be natural for them to answer that they rely on the improvement and expansion of public pensions and maintenance of the medical system. Recently, a ten-year plan for the welfare of the elderly was proposed by the government. The welfare policy of the elderly which was left behind was implemented as the pension system and medical treatment.

A welfare law for the elderly was revised in 1990 and the social welfare system was reconsidered. It now includes a range of social welfare services, the ideal quality of welfare service supply in society, improvement of home-nursing welfare, reinforcement of cooperation with home welfare, improvement of home welfare, high regard of the role of towns and villages and constructions of a new management system.

However, it is needless to say that the elderly demand independence and individuality as the policy progresses further, so

142

that the improvement of the pension system and the medical treatment system is necessary as a basic condition for the final stage.

Public pensions

A reform of the pension system in 1986 changed the national pension into a system which provides all people with a basic pension, while the conventional employee pension has become an income. This reform aimed to validate the standards and to establish the right of women's pension. The basic pension is not sufficient as welfare because it differs on certain conditions and the full amount is only 56,775 yen per month (1990).

Employee pensions such as welfare pensions and various mutual-aid pensions are supplied under the condition that a person was a full-time employee for a certain period of time. The average monthly allowance of the old-age (retirement) pension is from 132,000 yen (a welfare pension) to 195,000 yen (a mutual-aid union of local officials). On the other hand, the average monthly allowance of the national pension for a dependent spouse of an individual proprietor or an employee is 30,000 yen.

Elderly in Tokyo

The pension scheme in Japan is mainly developed for full-time workers. The big difference between them and others, such as individual proprietors, family employees, part-time workers and housewives, keeps the net income low for full-time working women with little work experience.

According to the results of the research on annual net incomes in the Tokyo area, the biggest proportion are the elderly, 65 years and over, with less than a 500,000 yen annual income with 23 per cent, followed by people with 1,000,000 - 2,000,000 yen (21 per cent) including both men and women. As age increases, the proportion of those with less than 500,000 yen per year increases. It reaches 35 per cent for over 80-year-olds. Distinguishing between men and women, men with less than 500,000 yen account for only 6 per cent, while the figure is 17 per cent for men over 80 years of age. The

143

biggest proportion of men's annual income is 2-3 million yen with 22 per cent. Moreover, 20 per cent of men get 3-5 million yen. On the other hand, 37 per cent of women earn less than 500,000 yen. The same amount for over 80-year-old women reaches 47 per cent, nearly half. The annual net income of the majority of women stops short of 2 million yen. The details are 22 per cent for 500,000 - 1,000,000 yen and 23 per cent for 1,000,000 - 2,000,000 yen.

Pensions are a little more than half of the total income of men and women, but they are less than half for men and more than half for women. Employment income is 20 per cent, and income from house and land rent is 13 per cent. The main source of income in different elderly male groups continues to be employment and salary in almost every fifth case in the oldest group (80 years and over) and in almost half the cases in the youngest group (65-69 years), on average one third of men over 64 years have employment as the main source of income (Table 2). With women, employment income is the main source of income in 17 per cent of cases, with 65 to 69 year-olds a little less than one third, and in the oldest group of 80 years and over still four per cent. Social assistance as the main source of income is higher with women (5 per cent) than with men (4 per cent), rising in the oldest age groups to 7.5 per cent for men and 7.0 per cent for women.

Nearly 20 per cent of old people whose main revenue is from their employment income get between 3 - 5 million yen. This is almost the same as the standard salaries for full-time workers. Some administrators and workers with special skills earn close to 10 million yen annually. The actual employment condition consists of full-time workers with 3 - 5 million yen (20 per cent), re-employed workers with 2 - 3 million yen (18 per cent), and part-time workers with 1 - 2 million yen (9 per cent).

The biggest proportion in pensions and widows' allowances is under 500,000 yen at 33 per cent, the next is 1.5 - 2 million yen at 25 per cent, and the third is 500,000 - 1,000,000 yen at 20 per cent.

The insufficient conditions provided by pensions lead to the need of maintenance compensation paid by family members or other contributors in the lowest income groups. This source of income has, however, lessened because of improvements in social legislation and changes in family relations.

Table 2
Source of main income by age, per cent

	Total	Wage and Salaries, Working fee	House rent, Land rent, Divided	Supply	Pension, Survivors' Pension	Allow-ances	Social assis-tance	Divers	D.K.
Total, age	100.0	20.0	13.1	2.8	55.4	0.5	4.5	0.9	2.9
65-69	100.0	30.6	12.1	1.9	45.0	0.7	2.6	0.2	6.9
70-74	100.0	20.8	12.7	2.2	56.8	0.5	4.3	1.9	0.8
75-79	100.0	12.9	13.2	3.1	64.4	0.3	5.4	-	0.7
80-	100.0	6.5	15.6	5.5	61.8	-	7.5	1.5	1.5
Male	100.0	32.8	8.3	0.4	44.8	1.2	3.7	0.8	7.9
65-69	100.0	39.8	8.4	-	30.1	2.4	-	1.2	18.1
70-74	100.0	43.1	3.4	1.7	43.1	1.7	3.4	1.7	1.7
75-79	100.0	24.1	10.3	-	58.6	-	5.2	-	1.7
80-	100.0	16.7	11.9	-	57.1	-	9.5	-	4.8
Female	100.0	17.0	14.2	3.3	57.9	0.3	4.7	0.9	1.7
65-69	100.0	28.3	13.0	2.4	48.7	0.3	3.2	-	4.1
70-74	100.0	16.7	14.4	2.2	59.3	0.3	4.5	1.9	0.6
75-79	100.0	10.1	13.9	3.8	65.8	0.4	5.5	-	0.4
80-	100.0	3.8	16.6	7.0	63.1	-	7.0	1.9	0.6

Source: 1990 Survey of Living Conditions of The Elderly in Tokyo, Tokyo 1991.

By international comparison, the employment rate of the elderly in Japan is very high. The low pension standard leaves many of the elderly with no other choice but to work.

Conclusions

As I have mentioned, the living conditions of the elderly tend to depend increasingly on pensions, and there are big differences between the various pension systems and between men and women in employment before old age. Pensions do not seem to provide appropriate security for the elderly. To make up for it, men continue to work in order to support themselves in old age with an employment income. Women's employment rate is low. They depend on pensions and widows' allowances, since their wages are small.

The employment income is an important part of the living expenditure for the elderly and they do not work just to work. The level of living conditions of aged women with disadvantages in pension provision and small employment incomes are inferior to that of men. For this reason we have to make an effort to reconstruct the life security system for aged women who have been kept behind with regard to opportunities in life because of child care, housework, care of parents and husband. Moreover, the tendency of women to be employed will strengthen in the Japanese society in the future. We hope that a thorough review of the social policies for family duties, such as child and nursing care, which have traditionally been done by women and which have not been considered a social problem in the past, will be conducted for the future.

References

Basic Survey of National Living (1989), Ministry of Health and Welfare, Tokyo (in Japanese).

1989 National Survey of Family Income and Expenditure (1989), Statistics Bureau, Management and Coordination Agency (in Japanese).

Poll on Savings (1990), The Saving and Publicity Central Committee, Tokyo (in Japanese).

1990 Survey of Living Conditions of the Elderly (1991), Tokyo Metropolitan Government, Tokyo (in Japanese).

8 Social policy planning and women in Japan

Ingrid Getreuer-Kargl

Introduction

Social policy planning in Japan concentrates, as I have contended elsewhere (Getreuer-Kargl 1990a; Getreuer-Kargl 1990b, 13-23), on measures concerning old age and the ageing of society. Both, old age and the ageing of society, are to a large extent a problem of and for women: 'the aged society closely relates to the women's problem' (Fukutake 1986, 141); in fact, 'one might say the so-called problem of the elderly is a women's problem' (Takahashi 1987a, 2). Given these premises one would expect the situation of women to be pivotal to social policy planning. This article attempts to throw light on the question to what extent, if indeed at all, this is the case.

In this context I shall restrict 'social policy planning' to basic policy outlines of the Ministry of Health and Welfare (*Kôsei-shô*) as they are reflected in the last three volumes of the White Paper on Health and Welfare (*Kôsei Hakusho*). In addition, I shall examine the 'women's problem'-consciousness of the social welfare experts I interviewed in the spring of 1988, as well as consider the discrepancies between government officials and a number of persons from the well-informed concerned public. Since these experts are among the opinion leaders as regards social welfare and/or the ageing society, their opinions reflect a potential for change. In the concluding chapter I shall discuss the extent to which social welfare policies really meet women's needs.

The main characteristics of the ageing society at present, as seen in the White Paper on Health and Welfare, are a rapid ageing process and a dramatic increase in old-old persons (75 years and over), as well as regional differences in the speed of ageing. The male-female ratio of persons aged 65-74 is 1:1.4, while of persons aged 75 and over it is 1:1.6 (Kôsei-shô 1989, 17), indicating a heavy surplus of elderly women, especially of old-old women. Life expectancy was 81.4 years for women and 75.6 for men born in 1987, as compared with 49.6 and 46.9 years respectively in 1935. (Kôsei-shô 1989, 8.)

Except for life expectancy, which is traditionally given separately for both sexes, the White Papers present the life situations of the elderly strictly gender-neutral, without any comment on the special conditions for elderly women. Only one passage, depicting in detail the portrait of the present (born 1916-1925) and future (born 1946-1955) elderly, considers the women's situation within the ageing society.

Old people of today underwent the shattering experience of World War II and quite a few women of this generation never had the opportunity to experience married life, because their potential mates died during the war: by the time the men of this generation reached their forties, 50 per cent of their contemporaries were already dead. Women married to men in self-employed enterprises worked side by side with their husbands, while the wives of employees stayed at home and raised their children or cared for their elderly parents. Now that they themselves are old, there is no one to look after them due to the decrease of three-generation households and the growing participation of women in society.[1] (Kôsei-shô 1989: 21-22.) Increasing participation of women in public affairs is documented by their higher level of education, their employment situation and the ratio of women possessing a driving licence. Only three out of 100 women of the older generation have received higher education compared with 21 out of 100 in the younger generation (for comparison: 13 vs. 29 per cent of men); moreover, six (eight) out of ten women (men) now enjoy the freedom of a driver's licence. This privilege was denied to all but five (men: 300) out of 1000 of the older generation (Kôsei-shô 1989, 23-25). 'It will be difficult', the Ministry perceptively states, 'to entrust human relations in the community to women or to expect wives to care for the parents' (Kôsei-shô 1989, 25).

Social policy planning by the Ministry of Health and Welfare

Policy-makers consider the remaining years of this century as a time of reforms which aim at a mature social security system ensuring a better quality of life. 'Japan's social security system no longer has to catch up with European and American standards but has reached a new stage of maturation where it is important that the demands of the population for 'quality of life' are met.' As the need for health and medical services and for care services is growing, improvements in the quantity and quality of the man-power supporting the social security system will be among the great challenges of social policy planning. (Kôsei-shô 1988, 1-2.) 'Basic policy ideas for the realization of a welfare society of longevity and targets of the policies'[2] are defined as follows:

(1) elderly people should not be considered objects of care and help, but rather persons who can contribute towards society by their knowledge and abilities;

(2) the idea of normalization (switching from institutional care for the elderly to ambulant and home care);

(3) the public sector is responsible for basic policies which must be supported by the population, but individual, family, regional and work place potential has to be made use of; and

(4) higher social security burdens for the population are inevitable, but they must not impair economic progress or society's vitality (Kôsei-shô 1989, 27).

The analysis of the White Papers shows that there is little diffe-rentiation between the situation of the male and female elderly and, consequently, no hint of sex-specific policies. It is generally known, however, what impact the growing participation of women in the labour market will have especially on family functions and the female social security manpower potential. Reforms of Japan's social security system during the past decade have primarily been aimed at reducing costs or at least alleviating the explosion of the social security budget (cf. also Tabata 1991, 24). Apart from the big pension reform and struggles to revamp the medical system, policies for a financially manageable social welfare system for the elderly seem to concentrate on:

(1) 'normalization' or promotion of home care;

(2) 'utilizing women in the house (*katei-fujin*)' or improvements in social security manpower; and

(3) 'diversification of services' or development of the private sector.

A closer look at these policies reveals that although they on the whole aim at giving elderly people a positive role in society, including the right to choose their own way of life, they are detrimental to women's right of self-determination.

(1) Normalization

The concept of 'normalization' is not new but it has gained importance during the last few years[3]. Normalization means a shift of focus to ambulant and home care services so as to create a society where elderly and handicapped persons can lead their lives with their families or in their own neighbourhoods (Kôsei-shô 1990, 64; Kôsei-shô 1989, 12). People who need social assistance, such as the mentally or physically handicapped, should not be looked upon as peculiar, but rather a society in which these people live should be considered normal (Kôsei-shô 1989, 12).

Some 600,000 people are bedridden and roughly the same number suffer from senile dementia (though some are counted in both categories) and their numbers are expected to rise to 1.8 million each by the year 2015 (Kôsei-shô 1988, 8-10; MHW 1988, 3[4]). Most of them still wish to be cared for by their family but the typical pattern of 'daughters or daughters-in-law caring for the parents' and 'wives caring for their husbands' is becoming unrealistic. This is all the more so, as in the case of the elderly caring for the elderly, the carers themselves might easily become objects of care because of excessive physical and mental burden. In order to help these families, there are plans to raise the number of short-stay-beds and of home-helps (*katei-hôshi*) from the present 27,105 (Kôsei-shô 1989, 237) to 50,000, and the number of day-service-centres to 10,000 by the year 2000. In addition, services provided by private enterprises and volunteers should be encouraged. (Kôsei-shô 1989, 42-45.) As for the most serious problem, senile dementia, the Ministry of Health and Welfare has

150

concentrated on research and has started a 'zero-strategy for the bedridden elderly' in 1990 aiming at minimizing the number of bedridden people in view of the fact that in Northern Europe the number of bedridden elderly is extremely small in comparison to Japan (Kôsei-shô 1990, 67).

Minimizing the institutionalization of persons who need some help is quite laudable but overdue. It is hoped that this will at the same time result in reduced social welfare expenditure, but whether this will come true is a moot question. According to Austrian estimates, adequate ambulant and home care services are not likely to be less expensive than stationary care (Dimensionen 1991). For the idea of normalization to be realized satisfactorily, a detailed concept of ambulant and home care services and ample manpower is a prerogative. At present, both are far from sufficient and seldom allow those who are completely dependent on these services to remain at home. Women are affected by this situation, because there are more bedridden or senile women than men (in 1984, 300,000 women were bedridden, as compared with 194,000 men; Eijingu 1986, 287). Since they have no one to take care of them (13.3 per cent of women over 65 lived in single households, as compared with 4.9 per cent of men; Kôsei-sho 1986, 46), they have to be placed in an institution and cannot go on leading a 'normal' life. Furthermore, it is women who will have to go on caring for the elderly (wives, daughters, daughters-in-law account for 72.6 per cent of all carers, while husbands, sons, sons-in-law account for only 7.3 per cent; Kôsei-sho 1986, 46), until and unless enough professionals are recruited and ambulant care facilities established. It is remarkable how reticent people are about asking men to join in the caring activity.

A functioning home care system requires efforts to keep elderly people as healthy as possible. Consequently, promotion of health preservation constitutes one of the policy measures. Considering the women's excessive burden of caring for the elderly, this must seem but an empty phrase to most female elderly.

(2) 'Utilizing women in the house (katei-fujin)' or improvements in social security manpower

A social welfare system with home care facilities enabling handicapped people to continue living at home involves a huge manpower. The Ministry of Health and Welfare points out that one out of every 18 gainfully employed workers is engaged in a social security related job. (MHW 1988, 5; Kôsei-shô 1988, 20.) In recent developments the steady increase in the number of volunteers (forming the 'informal sector') is quite noteworthy. They come from among old people themselves, students and housewives, those working for private social service organizations, and female social workers. 'Generally, however, social service volunteers from among the general public are still very few in this country compared with the Western countries. As a result, the number of people who belong to the 'informal sector' is far too small to meet the nation's social security needs, and this is posing a serious problem for the nation.' On the other hand, 'many social service workers lack the professional and technical competence needed in the care and rehabilitation of the sick'. (MHW 1988, 5; Kôsei-shô 1988, 20, 23, 29.) 'To meet the rapidly increasing need for diverse social services in the coming decades, it is necessary not simply to increase the number of medical doctors and nurses ('formal sector'), but to develop multi-layered manpower composed of local non-professional volunteers ('informal sector'). To accomplish this, housewives should be encouraged to actively participate in social services, machinery conducive [sic!] to the participation of the elderly and the business community must be created, and nationwide campaigns must be undertaken on a continuing basis to stimulate the sense of a shared social service.' (MHW 1988, 7; Kôsei-shô 1988, 33-37.)

Plans for a quantitatively adequate manpower centre around mobilizing housewives and the elderly themselves, preferably as volunteers but at least as low-paid home-helps and carers, to provide a well-qualified social security manpower at low cost. The idea of 'utilizing women in the house (*katei-fujin*) for social services' (Kôsei-shô 1988, 31) is an especially promising one as the Ministry details: As household burdens have lessened and women have gained more economic and emotional independence, housewives participate in public affairs to a growing extent, and the number of women who in fact seek employment and participate actively in social activities has risen considerably. Women's participation in public affairs has increased the need for social services since family functions, such as the upbringing of children, the care of the elderly and household chores, have been externalized. Therefore plans must be made to utilize housewives as supporters of social services. For example, the experience and knowledge of women who have cared for their old bedridden parents at home can be usefully employed in creating a system of community service. Already there are experiments whereby women at home are registered as community home-helps after a period of specialized training. Along with the rapid ageing, the need for nursing services will grow. It is especially important to secure the services of health visitors and public health nurses who provide counselling at home to back up medical home care for the bedridden elderly. As far as nurses are concerned, it is surmised that quite a number of registered nurses have quit their jobs and are now unemployed at home. The utilization of these unemployed nurses (public health nurses) as manpower for health visitor services in cooperation with medical facilities, or for visiting guidance schemes based on the Health for the Elderly Law is considered to be a key point in promoting medical home care for the bedridden elderly. Therefore the Ministry of Health and Welfare promotes nursing projects established in prefectures (employment mediation for registered nurses) and plans to dig up these 'submerged' nurses (public health nurses). Local public bodies also utilize the submerged nursing force and provide visiting guidance and other services for patients at home. (Kôsei-shô 1988, 31-32.)

The high ratio of women, already a characteristic of the social security manpower, is therefore likely to increase even apart from the 'tendency to rise even higher due to the participation of women in public affairs'. According to the 1985 population census, the ratio of female employees amounted to 50 per cent in the service industry as a whole, but jumped up to 79.4 per cent in the field of 'social insurance and social welfare' and to 72.3 per cent in the medical field. (Kôsei-shô 1988, 24.) When, in addition to employees, volunteers and family members are also taken into account, the social security manpower becomes overwhelmingly female. What actually changes for women is not so much the content of their assignment but their status. So far, most of them have cared for and nursed their old parent/s(-in-law) and their husbands without pay. If they now enter the social security manpower as professionals, they will be paid for doing the same for other people, using the money thus earned to buy services for their own elderly. The difference this makes for the carers — professionals as well as volunteers — should not be underrated, however: the work place is shifted to the outside world, while the home is more likely to offer respite.

A fully fledged home care system requires various services, as well as diverse qualifications in the people providing these services. However, they all have in common that they used to fall in the women's sphere. Providing food, clean linen and clothing, baths as well as nursing care in case of illness has been the women's responsibility and is designed to remain so by the will of the Ministry of Health and Welfare ('utilizing women in the home'). Instead of being offered a wider range of job openings, women are again to be confined to their traditional roles.

(3) Diversification of services or development of the private sector

Policy makers do not regard the present social security system and especially the social services as entirely satisfactory. This is due to the uniformity and inflexibility of the system. Future strategies for full-scale development of social security have to take into account the population's increasing and diversifying needs (Kôsei-shô 1989, 11). To meet these needs, plans have to be made in order to establish a sound system of private services, such as old people's homes which charge a fee of their residents (Kôsei-shô 1989, 12-13).

The public sector, it is argued, should provide services for persons unable to satisfy their needs at market prices, as well as services not or insufficiently offered by private enterprises. Such public services are to be supplemented by 'silver services', private enterprises catering for the needs of elderly people. There is some discussion regarding these 'silver services'; some people maintain that they are better able to meet the diversified needs of the elderly, easier to use and more efficient, while others criticize them for being expensive and only available to the well-to-do. In addition, the quality of private services is considered very inhomogeneous. (Kôsei-shô 1988, 155-157.)

People's demands for diversified services usually serve as an argument for decreasing (to a limited degree) the role of the state in social welfare and for promoting the engagement of the private sector, but the Ministry of Health and Welfare is also quite outspoken about the financial aspect: 'It has already become difficult, institutionally as well as financially, for the public sector alone to meet the demand [for care services for the elderly], and it has become necessary to create multiple sources that can provide such services. The basic approach to this problem should be the creation of a balanced mix of public and private services which incorporate the resources of the public sector, the market and the informal sector efficiently.' (MHW 1988, 8; Kôsei-shô 1988, 46-47.)

According to these policy plans, private enterprises are to play an important role in the establishment of the 'welfare society of longevity'. 'The increase in the number of infirm elderly in need of care and the diversification of their needs brought about by the wider availability of pension benefits, combined with the increase in nuclear families leading to the separation of the elderly from their children, have given rise to a growing demand for a 'silver service' (personal care of the infirm elderly). To support the growth of such a service, the government has made available professional guidance and low-interest loans to encourage the creation of commercial nursing homes of good quality, and now plans to institute an accreditation system to train and supply adequate numbers of qualified social welfare workers and welfare nurses' (MHW 1988, 16). The target of these silver services are single and couple households of the aged in need of personal care. In 1988 one third of the households receiving livelihood assistance were households of the elderly (Sômu-chô Tôkei-kyoku 1990, 587) and in 1985 82.1 per cent of the households of the aged receiving livelihood assistance were single households (Eijingu 1987, 314). In general, the financial means of the — eighty per cent female (Eijingu 1987, 165) — single households of the aged are restricted and probably not enough to allow these old people to resort to expensive silver services, especially as women's pension benefits are considerably smaller than men's. Consequently, it is mainly the couple households that profit from private services: every third man over 65 lives in a couple household, while the corresponding figure for women is not even one out seven. This policy measure benefits predominantly men.

Regions or communities also are to play a more active role in the ageing society, 'Local public bodies [...] are also actively involved in promoting social services by establishing volunteer centers and by offering their social welfare facilities as forums for public education in social welfare, or as places where social services can be offered. More recently, movements have emerged to organize local volunteers who can provide care services for the elderly, and this has attracted growing attention in regional communities' (MHW 1988, 16). Volunteer services tie up with the role that individuals are to play; in other words, elderly people are to 'contribute towards society by their knowledge and abilities'. As women's amateur and professional abilities are still linked with the 'social' field of caring for people and various activities in home making, tasks for which men have acquired little skill and less inclination, the concept of the 'contribution of the elderly' serves to tie women to their roles by making use of them as social welfare volunteers.

Behind the slogan 'maintain economic progress and society's vitality' — even though a higher social security burden is accepted as inevitable — stands the reluctance to raise taxes drastically; and the demand for 'equality among generations', or in other words, efforts to keep the economically active population's taxes and social insurance premiums at an acceptable level in proportion to their income. Also, the welfare budget has to be kept low so as not to impair economic progress. This can only mean that services are to be more expensive and public pension benefits only big enough to secure survival. Due to their insecure employment status, women's tax and premium contributions are small and hence they usually receive only public pensions (of the supplementary corporate pensions women benefit only indirectly through their husbands). Therefore, women experience only the negative aspects of low public social welfare expenditure, while men to some extent also enjoy the advantages of smaller taxes and social contributions.

There seems to be little awareness of the 'problem of the elderly as a women's problem' — one might rather contend that the Ministry of Health and Welfare deems the insubordination of women to their allegedly traditional roles within the family as the source of one of the major problems of the ageing society. Neither do suggestions by different committees and study groups exhibit consciousness of 'ageing as a women's problem'.

Experts' opinion on the ageing society and women[5]

In spring 1988 I conducted a series of standardized interviews with social welfare or ageing experts in Japan, asking questions concerning the awareness of the ageing society and welfare issues[6]. The 72

156

predominantly male experts (58 men, 14 women) were attached to ministries (= M) and prefectural offices (= P), research institutions and universities (= U), welfare organizations (= O), and mass media, political parties and labour unions (= MP). On the whole, the responses and opinions were male-oriented and argue at best a split mind concerning women's problems in the ageing society. The cited statements are not a selection but represent a complete range of explicit mentions of women in the questionnaires. These experts, too, had few comments and suggestions to make on women's situation in the ageing society.

Images of old people and the ageing society

Old people were characterized as having long life-experience and failing bodily powers, the ageing society was associated with a high percentage of elderly, a matured and settled or else a dark, gloomy society that has lost its vitality and poses an excessive burden on the economically active population. Someone associated 'a society of widows' (63, MP, m[7]) with the ageing society, another deplored in this context the lack of public care systems: 'special nursing homes for the aged have only a capacity for one per cent of the aged. In Japan, care in the family still prevails and that is an enormous burden especially on women' (68, MP, m). Two thirds believed that the ageing of the population would influence economy and labour practices. Retirement age would rise, life-long employment and seniority system change, sliver industries would develop, but more significant would be the stagnation of economy and the loss of economic vitality. 'More social roles for women' (3, P, m) were optimistically expected, which might perhaps be specified as follows: 'in respect to women's labour force participation, the ageing society might well be a cheerful one if, due to the changes in the service sector, women lead an animated life as waitresses, bus and other hostesses or stewardesses' (36, O, f). Other major consequences of the ageing were seen in a change from a youth culture into a culture of the aged, in a heavy financial burden — especially on the economically active population — resulting from social security expenditures, and generally in a loss of vitality, and stagnation.

The most pressing problems of the ageing society were considered to relate to (1) medical insurance and the medical care system, (2) pensions and financial security, (3) *ikigai* or meaning in life, (4) employment and work, and (5) care services and manpower. The medical as well as the employment and care sector were expected to become less important in the 21st century, while pensions and especially meaning in life were expected to gain in importance. When asked to give the three most important problems of the ageing society at present and in the 21st century, three of the interviewed experts cited women's problems: 'at present: 1. no big problems; 2. most elderly live in relatively favourable circumstances; 3. if one dares to mention it: one third of single old women inevitably leading a hard life will be a problem' (55, U, m). '1. income and flats for single old women' (51. U, f) and in the 21st century: '1. to have enough children; and 2. institutions for the aged are insufficient, which is a women's problem' (69, MP, m).

Similarly, the expectations of the population with regard to the role of the state mainly concerned income security and financial independence for the elderly, measures for the bedridden, demented and single elderly, including a better home care system and improvement of the standard of the medical care system.

Major fields of concern

In the course of the interviews, four areas[8] of concern emerged as dominant themes: income security, care services and manpower, characteristics and necessary reforms of social security, and meaning in life (*ikigai*). They will be briefly discussed in the context of the awareness of women's situation.

Regarding income for the elderly, state guaranteed public pensions at a higher level than today were almost unanimously considered the desirable main source of income. Savings ranked second with the majority of the interviewees, while corporate pensions ranked second with a minority; corporate pensions or, to a lesser degree income from work, ranked third. This is a male point of view, for while public pensions should benefit both women and men alike, savings, corporate pensions and income from work as a subsidiary income are probably available to few women, except in a functioning marriage relationship and even there only for a part. (Incidentally, taking only couples into consideration could be seen as one of the main characteristics of the debate on income security, pensions and related issues in Japan). Single or divorced and to some extent widowed women too face a situation in which there are no concepts to guarantee them a sufficient income. Similarly, in the discussion of labour-related problems, it has frequently been stated that the labour market would have to be opened to elderly people, and that the lifetime employment and seniority system would have to change, but women's specific labour conditions (part-time work, early retirement clauses, insufficient social security provisions, low wages) were not mentioned. The above mentioned 'income for single old women' as the most important present problem of elderly women had to go.

The necessity of ample care services was somewhat disputed since at the same time the desirability of old people remaining in their homes for as long as possible was stressed, as was the fact that women bore the burden of care. Actually, this was the one specifically female problem in the ageing society which most experts were aware of. One might cynically contend, however, that what aroused them was not the intolerable situation of the carers today, but rather the unpleasant possibility that they might themselves have to cope without a carer in their old age. They generally believed that elderly bedridden people ought to be able to stay at home (78.6 per cent), while in the case of senile dementia home care was largely considered unrealistic with only four out of ten experts opting for the home as a desirable living environment. When staying at home, social services were considered a condition sine qua non, for no one thought that the families should care for their elderly unaided, whereas six out of ten agreed to the desirability of enlisting social services. In other words, though the family was seen as the main responsible party for the care of elderly people, they were believed to be shouldering more than their share already, while the state, neighbours and community were not considered sufficiently engaged yet. Two female experts touched on the increasing participation of women in the labour market: 'so far, society has counted on women to bear the care for the aged but the future society will be one in which the state and enterprises must willy-nilly take the care for the elderly on to themselves as women will use their abilities outside the home in society' (45, U, f). 'the ideal aged society is one in which every one who wants to work, young and old, men and women, can work' (50, U, f).

What ministry officials called 'utilizing women in the home' was seen as a characteristic of the Japanese type of welfare: 'Japan's welfare society is characterized by the use of women's cheap labour and low level of welfare services' (36, O, f). Others mentioned women in the context of their function as carers: the terminus 'Japanese model of a welfare state' was believed to express the 'importance of making the family responsible for the care of the elderly. Positive aspects: lower public expenses; negative aspects: economical and psychological burden on women' (27, M, f); or, conversely, 'priority is given to institutional welfare with classification and isolation. Recently, however, bonds between family and community have strengthened and welfare in the community and at home are increasing. Carers are mainly wives and daughters-in-law' (8, P, m), and 'it is an 'internment' type of welfare, with welfare institutions and medical facilities, which has developed as a consequence of the breakdown of the family system and the increase in families with both husband and wife working' (11, P, m). Japan was seen as a 'welfare society in which people are not accepted as individuals but are pinned down to specifically Japanese sentiments. This is exemplified in that the feudal remains of the traditional concept, to make families, especially women, responsible for maintenance and care of the aged, could not be erased' (33, O, m). Even the widespread cliché of the emotional superiority of the Japanese welfare model was challenged: 'Western models are very expensive, therefore plans [have been made] to carry welfare back into the home. Formerly, there was a distinct division of labour: women were at home, men employed; now that women are working outside, the old model does not work any more. There is a great misunderstanding: in many descriptions, all old people are institutionalized and the relations between old people and their children are cold. This is not true, family members frequently visit their elderly and also try to live in the vicinity. In Japan there are many problems and frictions between mother-in-law and daughter-in-law' (67, MP, m).

A higher level of social security, especially better welfare services, was clearly called for and there were few illusions about the financial consequences. On the question of whether to keep the social security budget at the present level of the national income or to reduce the per capita social security benefits, only 1.4 per cent opted for the reduction of benefits while 61.1 considered a higher social security budget as inevitable. Exactly half of the persons interviewed considered the present amount of taxes and premiums

160

insufficient, while only one out of eight considered it too high, the majority agreeing that persons in the upper income class bore too low a burden.

Another key factor of the ageing society was life planning for the longer retirement period: to find a meaning in life (*ikigai*) after retirement, the elderly should either be granted an opportunity to go on working for as long as they wanted to, or else they should not concentrate on their jobs only but should establish other interests in good time. In this the female life cycle is ignored: in general, women retire earlier and are seldom totally absorbed in their jobs. Only a few remarks on women were made in this context and they were contradictory and not very appreciative of women's concerns. 'In comparison with other countries, women pay less attention to the region and have fewer friends; but because of strong family bonds they are not necessary anyway. Men are deeply involved in their companies but not at all in the community; women work a lot in the house and have few outside contacts' (52, U, m). 'It is necessary to establish a meaning in life before retirement but there may be conflicts between husband and wife: I want to go into the country and do gardening and reading, my wife will not come with me because she is involved with neighbourhood work' (71, MP, m).

As in the White Papers discussed above, women were mentioned mainly in connection with their function as carers or their increasing participation in the labour market. While generally men's problems, life styles and situations are the starting point of reflections on policies and solutions for the ageing society, the excessive burden placed on women by their role as carers of the bedridden or senile elderly is not ignored and promotion of social services to ease their lot ranks high on the priority list. Their traditional role as homemakers and carers, however, is not really questioned. A female expert acknowledged the underprivileged position of women and included them in her wishes for an ideal society: 'the ideal society for the aged is a society that is also ideal for the handicapped elderly, children, women and other people considered socially weak; a completely egalitarian society without discrimination by age, sex or income' (47, U, f). Thus, even though there are disagreements between the experts interviewed and the officials on policies for the elderly and the aged society, they hardly ever comprise policies for women or the absence of such. If

161

Japanese women are dissatisfied with their position in official plans for social security, they will have to find another lobby to support their claims than welfare experts, presuming the above opinions are at all representative.

Social welfare as fulfilling needs

Welfare (*fukushi*), it has been argued, is the ideal condition in which four basic human needs are satisfied, namely (1) the need for economic welfare, (2) the need for health, (3) the need for emotional welfare, and (4) the need for self-realization (Takahashi 1987a, 6-7). In regard to women, to what extent does the Japanese state contribute towards satisfying these needs or creating an atmosphere in which others (companies, communities, private organizations) are stimulated to satisfy them?

(1) The need for economic welfare

Independent income (e.g. excluding financial support from children) of old people derives mainly from three sources: pensions, income from work and savings or private insurances. 'Important factors concerning economic stability in old age are public pensions, private provisions and the question of up to what age people want to work: half of the Japanese men want to work until the age of 65, a desire that must be gratified with regard to the vitality of economy and society' (Kôsei-shô 1989, 35). Pensions already account for more than half of the income in the households of the aged (Kôsei-shô 1990, 129) and are likely to rise in importance as pension schemes mature. The 1985 pension reform established a two-tier system with a basic pension for all[9] and an income-related pension for employees, and assured, among other things, that everybody including housewives would receive a pension of their own by the year 2025 at the latest. This pension alone is not sufficient to live on but it is supposed to be augmented by the income-related part of the pension under one of the employees' pension schemes and even, ideally, by an additional voluntary company pension.

Income-related pensions require contributions during a considerable time (standard: 35-40 years) of employment. Women average

162

7.1 years of employment and three out of ten female workers are non-regular workers, mostly part-timers. Women often discontinue work upon marriage, childbirth and for child care, and return to work when the burden of child care has decreased, often re-employed as 'part-timers' (MOL 1990, 5-6, 9, 11). Women's insecure and discontinuous employment career leaves them little hope for any substantial income-related pension and low wages reduce their chances even further. To the average worker family net income, wives contributed less than one tenth, and even of the average net monthly income per dual-income household, wives earned only one fifth. This is not astonishing since part-timers, for example, that is non-regular worker averaging 22 six-hour working days a month, are paid an average 642 yen per hour (MOL 1990, 8). The negligible amount of female income-related pensions is indirectly admitted in the Ministry of Health and Welfare calculations of the standard pension. Standard pensions (basis: 1989, figures according to Kôsei-shô 1990, 132) are calculated per household (= married couple) and are composed of the basic pensions of husband and wife (55,500 yen each) plus the husband's income-related pension (84,492 yen) — an income-related pension of the wife is never even mentioned.

Actually, the situation of employees' wives without or with only a small income has improved under the new pension system. They will receive a basic pension of their own while their insurance premiums (for the basic pension) are paid by all contributors to the Employees' Pension Insurance in acknowledgement of the social value of women's household work and child raising. Regularly employed women pay their contributions to the Employees' Pension Insurance like men and so are paying their share of non-working wives' premiums, while performing household chores and child care duties like all other women. This inequality is enhanced by the fact that after the husband's death these women have to choose between their own income-related pension and the survivor's pension after their husbands. Giving up their own, usually smaller pension means that they have paid premiums without benefiting from it in the form of pension. (cf. Motozawa 1988, 110-113.)

This discrimination of regularly employed married, divorced or single women may be taken as a strong pressure upon women not to compete with men in the labour force (but content themselves with badly paid part-time work) and to mind their household duties and care of children and the elderly. Possibly the reformers had the concept of 'utilizing women in the home' in their minds when they thought of these provisions. Public and publicly encouraged pensions will allow men to retire from work and enjoy their old age in relatively comfortable circumstances, whereas their wives, most of whom have also worked to some extent outside the home, have to continue cooking and washing for them and even nursing them to earn their share of the pension.

Pensions thus do not fulfil women's needs for economic security, neither does their income from work. It may be added that women have for long been (and still are?) confronted with a lower retirement age than men: in 1985, 15.6 per cent of enterprises with a set retirement age had a separate system by sex (MOL 1985, 3), but different retirement ages have now been declared illegal by the Equal Opportunity Law. Still, the primary responsibility for the care of aged parents, when investigated, proved to be affecting women's employment: 'In case of women, around 40 per cent of those who had been working were obliged to quit or change jobs to take care of their old parents' (MOL 1990, 15). In 1980, almost one million women over 65 (half the number of men) belonged to the active workforce, most of them in agriculture and fishing, sales occupations and handicrafts, production process and labour, three out of ten working for more than 43 hours a week, which though less than men's working hours, is quite considerable (Eijingu 1986, 237, 245).

(2) The need for health

To satisfy the need for health, it is first of all important to provide for an environment conductive to health preservation and to remove factors detrimental to people's health. Without attempting to enumerate all relevant factors as known at present, attention must be paid to one big difference between the sexes: men suffer from overwork (the well-known *karôshi* — death from overwork — syndrome), women (much less publicly) from multiple burdens, including overburden of care.

The traditional concept of 'man the wage earner' and 'woman the householder' is still strong and women have to comply with it. Women working full time spent 7 hours and 45 minutes on commuting and working, and another 3 hours 31 minutes on

164

housework, child care and shopping. Their husbands commuted and worked for 10 hours and 1 minute but spent only 8 minutes (!) on housework, child care and shopping. (MOL 1990, 12.) This leaves wives with almost one hour less leisure time than their much-pitied work-addicted husbands. As for persons caring for old relatives, they average 60 years of age[10] and yet have to do heavy work like giving a bath to the person they are caring for. More than half complain of backache, bodily fatigue, want of sleep, blood pressure irregularities and having no time for themselves or even for consulting a doctor (Okamura 1987, 53-54; Asahi Shinbun, satellite edition, 1987-09-05, 13). It has even been said that 'each year that a bedridden person lives longer takes a year off of the carer's life' (Asahi Shinbun, satellite edition, 1988-09-20, 13). Higher life expectancy makes more women prone to illness and incapacitating diseases, and therefore special attention should be paid to their health maintenance. This is not the case, however. The planned promotion of home care services would benefit women shouldering the burden of care, but this would happen at the cost of having to do similar services outside the home on a more or less voluntary basis ('utilizing women in the home', promoting volunteer activities).

More attention is paid to men's health preservation, because men are identified with their work place and this has led many enterprises to grant their employees surplus social benefits from which working women are excluded except for the minority of full-time employed women. 'In an effort to help the growing number of elderly workers keep fit and in good shape while actively employed as well as after retirement on annuity, the government actively encourages 'senior plans' (projects for planning and developing welfare facilities at the corporate level) by making such projects eligible for social welfare loans from Welfare Annuity funds' (MHW 1988, 16).

Women who are taken ill and need care are disadvantaged compared with men. Men in need of care usually have their spouses to care for them, the intimacy and mutual dependence of matrimony making such care a fact of life and a more or less integral part of wifely duties. If not in institutions, women are mostly cared for by their daughters-in-law whose time they can lay no claim to. Having better financial means, men can choose to buy services if necessary or to enter expensive private homes or *kea-*

tsuki-apâto (flats with attached care facilities) for the aged. Consequently, they can more independently decide about their lives, even when disabled or bedridden. Women have to rely on their children or on public services and institutions and to take what is provided for them.

(3) The need for emotional welfare

To most people emotional welfare is linked to satisfying human relationships and certainly not a direct responsibility of social policies. The problem of the elderly is related to their 'condition of 'dependence and isolation" (Takahashi 1987b, 19). What can reasonably be expected of social policies is that they remove structural obstacles to functioning human relationships.

According to recent research results, couple relationships gain importance: three out of four persons between 50 and 69 wanted to enjoy life as a couple for as long as both partners were healthy; only one out of four believed unconditionally in living together with their children (Kôsei-shô 1988, 14-18). Higher life expectancy of women and higher age of the husband generate quite different family conditions for men and women. In 1989, even in the highest age group (85 and over), almost half of the male population were married as compared to only 5.3 per cent of the female; in other words, exactly nine times as many men were still married (Sômu-chô Tôkei-kyoku 1990, 44). The husband's intense involvement with his job and the wife's triple burden of homemaking, child raising and outside work leave little time for communication and shared activities for which reason women appear to draw little emotional support from a couple relationship. Married women are not more satisfied with life and do not show fewer symptoms of depression than widowed women (Kawaai 1984, 43); on the contrary, the more leisure time on the husband's side diminishes marital satisfaction on the wife's side (Sodei & Tsuzuki 1985, 76). Partner-orientation, it might be concluded, is growing but the modes of life together have still to be established. Social policies might contribute towards more successful couple relationships by offering guidelines for a new kind of couple-oriented life. This is not the case, however, as the official policies rather seem inclined to maintain women's traditional roles and, consequently, the division of male and female spheres.

Seven out of ten women aged 65 and over (six out of ten men) live together with their children (Yoda 1985, 12). In view of the expressed wish to enjoy an independent life as a couple, it may be suspected that this is not always the desired way of living, but rather one dictated by necessity. According to a Tokyo study, most old people living together with their children were financially dependent on them. Sixty per cent lived below and another 13 per cent on the poverty line[11] (Honma 1985, 42ff). On the other hand, the extremely small homes and the sons' frequent job transfers to other parts of the country often prevent cohabitation, even if both parties would like it. Especially among people in the lower income brackets there are many old women living alone, since the living conditions and small incomes do not allow cohabitation (Nasu 1981, 47).

Almost two thirds (Sômu-chô Tôkei-kyoku 1990, 44) of the elderly women are without a partner and many of them, 13.3 per cent of elderly women in all (4.9 per cent of men; Yoda 1985, 12), live alone. Four out of five one-person households of the aged are female. Loneliness is especially hard to bear for widows with small incomes (Kawaai 1984, 43), as poverty tends to confine people to their homes. It might well be that women's life situation motivates them to participate in volunteer activities as a cure for loneliness. The official policy of promoting volunteer activities could be seen as an aid to women to find new meaning in life, but in the absence of alternatives it has an air of exploitation.

(4) The need for self-realization (ikigai)

'Individuals themselves must prepare for old age, namely take care to preserve their health, set up relationships and ensure a meaning in life. It is important not to concentrate solely on the work place but to spend time in the local community as well. Enterprises, too, must contribute: some enterprises already offer courses on planning life after retirement', the Ministry of Health and Welfare counsels (Kôsei-shô 1989, 30-31). Advising people not to concentrate solely on the work place and adjuring enterprises to contribute towards life planning have no direct relevance for women. Men's life planning might be seen as a one-way road of work and employment: they work well into old age, eight out of ten until 64, two thirds until 69 and nearly half until 74 years of age, whereas only four out of ten women work until 64 and one fourth until 69 (Kargl 1987, 260-262).

Ikigai measures centre around the work place, either as employment promotion for the elderly or as preparatory courses for the time after retirement. Women, whose main reason in life is still seen in child-bearing and raising, are faced with the need for re-orientation much earlier: their youngest child marries and their first grandchild is born when they are in their mid-fifties and their husbands will still work for another five years (cf. Kargl 1987, 182-183). After having raised her children, the remaining 30 years in a way constitute an excess of lifetime for the woman. However, the future may bring further changes in her life, when the husband retires, when for financial or physical reasons they move to live together with their children, and finally when her husband dies. One wonders whether women find it possible to plan their life in old age, since it is to a large degree determined by factors outside their influence.

Women are hampered in preserving their health by having to care for their old husbands or parents in the absence of functioning public care services; they have little chance of setting up relations with their husbands due to the men's long working hours which women cannot influence; and many have little time to maintain relations with friends and neighbours because of their multiple burdens. Only part-time jobs are available for women after the break for child-bearing and raising and even these are dependent on the economic situation. In addition, women have to cope with their own as well as their husbands' illness and disability, and they are financially dependent on their husband and children. All these factors narrow the margin of independent decisions but are significantly missing in the discussion of a 'meaning in life' for old people. Women will have to find their own meaning in life without any help from official institutions. But perhaps they have already succeeded in doing that without all the hue and cry made about men?

'The problem is that, faced with the fate of ageing, society ought to provide assistance but does not' (Takahashi 1987a, 7). This is probably true for all, but if assistance is provided at all, it goes to men. Women have yet a long way to go before their needs are even recognized, much less taken care of.

Notes

1. 'Participation of women in public affairs' (*josei no shakai shinshutsu*) is translated elsewhere as 'women joining the labour market' (MHW 1988, 4) and apparently stands for the fact or fear of women's increasing reluctance to put their 'family functions' above their occupational careers.
2. *Chôju-fukushi shakai o jitsugen suru tame no shisaku no kihon-teki kangaekata to mokuhyô ni tsuite.* October 1988.
3. 'Normalization' was a terminus coined by a Danish movement of parents of 'mentally retarded' persons in 1959. In the 1970s it began to attract attention in Japan as well and has recently become a popular word in the mass media, as well as with welfare specialists and politicians. It implies that old, young and handicapped people should be able to lead their ordinary ('normal') lives in society and that segregating the aged and handicapped in institutions is abnormal. From now on it will be the leading concept in social welfare. (Ichibangase 1987, 411.)
4. Information has been taken from the original White Paper, but for convenience's sake I use the English summary rather than my own whenever possible.
5. Quoted statements have been taken directly from the questionnaires, for the other statements compare: Getreuer-Kargl 1990b, 73-75, 88-93, 104, 108-109, 117, 125, 127-128, 137-140, 150, 153, 193.
6. This study has been published as: Ingrid Getreuer-Kargl, *Ende der Dynamik? Eine Expertenbefragung zur Alterung der japanischen Gesellschaft*. Wien: Institut für Japanologie 1990 (= Beiträge zur Japanologie 28).
7. The numbers and letters in brackets refer to: the number of the questionnaire, to the institution the expert was affiliated to (capital letter), and to the sex (m = male, f = female).
8. Excluding the very complex issues of medical care and pension systems which are only of marginal relevance to this paper, especially as no reference was made to women.
9. Contribution to the basic pension scheme amounting to 8,400 yen per month in 1989 (Asahi Shinbun, satellite edition, 1989-01-25: 9) is obligatory with the corresponding right to a monthly pension of 55,000 yen from the age of 65 after a 40-year contribution period.

10. According to another study, one third each are in their fifties and over 60; Okamura 1987, 49-50.
11. 'Below the poverty line' related to persons with an income less than 140 per cent, 'on the poverty line' to persons with an income between 140 and 200 per cent of the sum granted under the Livelihood Protection Law.

References

Bando-Sugahara, Mariko (1982), 'Family circumstances of senior citizens', Naoshiro Yashiro et al. *Japan's rapidly aging population*. Foreign Press Center, Tokyo.

Dimensionen (1991), *Die Welt der Wissenschaft. Altenhilfe in Österreich 1988-2011. Bestandsaufnahme und zukünftige Entwicklung*, Gestaltung: Inge Smolek, Study of the Austrian Institute for Regional Planning.

Eijingu, sôgô kenkyû sentâ nenkan henshu iin-kai (ed.) (1986), *Kôrei-ka shakai kiso shiryô nenkan*, Eijingu Sôgô Sentâ, Tôkyô.

Eijingu, sôgô kenkyû sentâ nenkan henshu iin-kai (ed.) (1987), *Kôrei-ka shakai kiso shiryô nenkan*, Eijingu Sôgô Sentâ, Tôkyô.

Fukutake, Tadashi (1986), *Fukutake Tadashi chosaku-shû hokan*, Tôkyô Daigaku Shuppan-sha, Tôkyô.

Getreuer-Kargl, Ingrid (1990a), 'Alterung als zentrales sozialpolitisches Problem der Gegenwart und Zukunft', *Nachrichten der Gesellschaft für Natur- und Völkerkunde Ostasiens*, Hamburg 145-146.

Getreuer-Kargl, Ingrid (1990b), *Ende der Dynamik? Eine Expertenbefragung zur Alterung der japanischen Gesellschaft*, Institut für Japanologie, Beiträge zur Japanologie 28, Wien.

Honma, Shingo (1985), 'Dôkyo setai ni okeru rônin, ko sedai no keizai-teki kyôdô, izon kankei ni tsuite', *Shakai rônen-gaku* 22.

Ichibangase, Yasuko (1987), 'Shakai fukushi yôgo', *Gendai yôgo no kiso chishiki '87*.

Kargl, Ingrid (1987), *Old Age in Japan. Long-term Statistics*. Institut für Japanologie, Beiträge zur Japanologie 24, Wien.

Kawaai, Chieko (1984), 'Haigû-sha to no shibetsu go ni okeru rônen-ki josei no jinsei', *Shakai rônen-gaku* 20.

Kôsei-shô (1986), *Kôsei hakusho Shôwa 60-nenpan. Chôju shakai ni mukatte sentaku suru*, Kôsei Tôkei Kyôkai, Tôkyô.

Kôsei-shô (1988), *Kôsei hakusho Shôwa 62-nenpan. Shakai hoshô o ninau hitobito — shakai sâbisu wa kô tenkai suru*, Kôsei Tôkei Kyôkai, Tôkyô.

Kôsei-shô (1989), *Kôsei hakusho Shôwa 63-nenpan. Arata na kôrei-shazô to katsuryoku aru chôju-fukushi shakai o mezashite. Kôsei-shô sôsetsu 50-shûnen kinen-gô*, Kôsei Tôkei Kyôkai, Tôkyô.

Kôsei-shô (1990), *Kôsei hakusho Heisei gannen-pan. Chôju shakai ni okeru kodomo, katei, chiiki*, Kôsei Tôkei Kyôkai, Tôkyô.

White Paper on Health and Welfare, 1987 (1988), *Workers Supporting the Social Security System and the Image of Social Service of the Future (summary)*, Ministry of Health and Welfare (MHW), Foreign Press Center, Tokyo.

Results of 1985 Employment Management Survey (summary) (1985), Ministry of Labor (MOL), Foreign Press Center, Tokyo.

The Labor Conditions of Women 1989 (summary) (1990), Ministry of Labor (MOL), Foreign Press Center, Tokyo.

Motozawa, Miyoko (1988), 'Die Rentenversicherung in Japan — das neue Rentenversicherungssystem der Grundrente mit Zusatzsicherung', *Zeitschrift für ausländisches und internationales Arbeits- und Sozialrecht (ZIAS)*, 2.

Nasu, Soichi (1981), 'The Modern Significance of Research into Welfare for the Aged', Fukutake Tadashi et al.: *The Japanese family*, Foreign Press Center, Tokyo.

Naikaku, Sôri Daijin Kanbô Rôjin Taisaku-shitsu (1984), *Korei-sha mondai kankei shiryô-sho*, Naikaku Sôri Daijin Kanbô Rôjin Taisaku-shibu, Tokyo.

Natsuki, Shizuko (1981), 'Facts and fallacies of old age', *Japan Echo* 8.

Okamura, Kiyoko (1987), 'Rôjin no kea shisutemu to josei shûgyô-sha no sho-mondai (dai-ikkai)', *Kôreika-shakai to josei. 21-seiki no Nihon shakai o kangaeru kôza kôen kiroku kara*. [Tanashi-machi]: Tanashi Shiritsu Chûô Kômin-kan (= 62 chiiki kôza shiryô).

Sodei, Takako and Tsuzuki, Kayo (1985), 'Teinen taishoku go fûfu no kekkon manzoku-do', *Shakai rônen-gaku* 22.

Sômu-chô Tôkei-kyoku (ed.) (1990), *Dai-yonjû-kai Nihon tôkei nenkan. Heisei 2-nen*, Nihon Tôkei Kyôkai, Tôkyô.

Tabata, Hirokuni (1991), 'The Japanese Welfare State: Its Structure and Transformation', *Annals of the Institute of Social Science* 32.

Takahashi, Masato (1987a), 'Kôrei-ka shakai to josei', *Kôreika-shakai to josei. 21-seiki no Nihon shakai o kangaeru kôza kôen kiroku kara.* [Tanashi-machi]: Tanashi Shiritsu Chûô Kômin-kan (= 62 chiiki kôza shiryô).

Takahashi, Masato (1987b), 'Josei no rôgo to kazoku ni tsuite', *Kôreika-shakai to josei. 21-seiki no Nihon shakai o kangaeru kôza kiroku kara.* [Tanashi-machi]: Tanashi Shiritsu Chûô Kômin-kan (= 62 chiiki kôza shiryô).

Yoda, Seiichi (1985), *1985-nendo hôgaku tokkô, Kôrei-sha o meguru hô to seisaku shiryô-shû.* (manuscript)

9 The elderly and institution in Japan – the case of institutional care in Tokyo

Raija Hashimoto

Introduction

'*Ningen, shinu koto wa tayasui.*
Shikashi, kokoro, utsukushiku ikitogeru koto wa muzukashii.'

To live and then die — easy.
But to live an entire life beautifully — difficult.

> By Mr. O., a resident of Shisei Home, at the age of 85, one year before his death, in his honoured memory

So wrote a wise old man, a resident of Shisei Home, Tachikawa City, a suburb of Tokyo, a few years ago. This tall and slender, highly intelligent and well-liked person by co-residents and staff, spent the last ten years of his life at the *Keihi* A (low-pay home) type part of the above-mentioned home, in the shade of cherry trees and with a view of the Tama River flowing gently past. Perhaps with the inspiration of the scenery around, he, the former editor in a publishing company, was amazingly busy with writing. He, among other things, helped the director of the home publish the Home Diary, a bulletin featuring happenings at the home and appearing six times a year.

Mr. O. was an active member of numerous hobby groups, among them the Ikebana (flower arrangement) class, a pastime usually not very popular among men. He was regularly visited by his children,

173

who, in turn, were active in the Association of The Relatives of Shisei Home Residents. The agony of his private life, a divorce he had experienced, seemed to have been forgotten. A gentleman who wore a suit and a necktie every day, he was mentally active and sane till the very end. Great was the feeling of loss at his passing away of a stroke.

Mr. O. was one of those Japanese elderly who had chosen, or, because of the family situation, had been compelled to choose a Home for the Aged as his last earthly home.

As in 1990 about 1.6 per cent, or 220,000, of the 14 million elderly in Japan, i.e. those over 65 years of age, lived in about 3000 government-subsidized shelters for the elderly. Besides, there are around 150 privately-run homes that offer luxurious facilities at steep prices. This so-called 'Silver Industry' ('silver' meaning aged), business making use of old people's money, is a rapidly growing sector and drawing much attention.

Society then — now

Now Japan is in a phase of history that it has never faced before: a country with a high technology as well as a changed population, changed family structure and functions, women's movement and peoples increased lifetime. With rapid progress of medicine and nutrition the Japanese are now the longest-living nation in the world. The rate of the very old is rapidly growing, which is putting enormous stress on families and the society as a whole.

Through urbanization and the abolition of the *ie* system after the Second World War the Japanese family has gone through an enormous change. The size of family has become smaller. The birth rate has dropped being now one of the lowest in the world. According to a 1990 survey an average Japanese woman gives birth to 1.53 children.

With the country's rapid economic growth, life styles have changed and the 'nuclear family' is becoming the norm, resulting in more and more elderly living alone. In 1987, 32 per cent of all the households consisted of senior citizens living alone or as couples.

A prominent Japanese statesman said some time ago, reflecting ideology of the past, that the pillar of Japanese old people's welfare lies and should lie on the three-generations-living-together. His ideas stirred the nation and raised much ado by both the public and people working in the social field.

However, looking from the world's point of view, the Japanese family still stands on a platform of its own. As in 1960 90 per cent of those over 65 lived with their married children, in 1985 the figure was still as high as 69.5 per cent. The estimate for the year 2000 is 60.3 per cent and for 2025 52.1 per cent. It is going slowly down, but still hanging relatively high. Vaguer than before but, nevertheless, the ancient social code of settling the problems of aging inside the extended family that the statesman emphasized is still there.

But should old people's welfare be looked from this angle in the future, too? Can the family of tomorrow, or even today, alone look after the ever older and weaker old people? The answer seems to be 'no'. Even though the idea of various generations living together seems ideal in many ways, in the new circumstances it is not enough. The care of the whole family should be discussed, say the writers of Rojinfukushiron, (Discussions on Old People's Welfare). In order not to make the *yomesan* (wife of son) stop working outside home, which she has started like many of her fellow sisters in Japan in recent years, to look after the elderly, as often is the case, a new type of care must be realized in Japan, too, as for instance in the Scandinavian countries. 'The old people's problems and ethics of respect for the aged cannot cope with the problems of today', say the writers of Rojinfukushiron. 'The problem of aging is the problem of the whole society.'

Man then — now

During the last 40 years or so, the life span of the Japanese has gone through an enormous rise. In the first Yearly Report of the Ministry of Health and Welfare (1947) the average life span of Japanese women was 54.0 years and men 50.1 years. In 1990 the figures were respectively 81.8 and 75.9, the top position in the world, even surpassing Sweden and Iceland. The number of elderly, the population of those over 65 years of age is around 14.3 million making up 11.6 per cent of the whole population (1989). 94 per cent of them live at home and at least 50-60 per cent have some sort of health problem. In September 1991 there were 3625 centenarians or older in Japan.

175

The old people of today were people born before or at the beginning of the Showa Era (the era of the reign of Emperor Hirohito that lasted from 1926 to 1989). They are people who have experienced severe changes in society and in their own lives: the Great Tokyo Earthquake, the military uprising in the 1930s, the Second World War, poverty and hunger, change from an agricultural society to an industrial one, the Occupation and the Land Reform, the huge industrialization and urbanization of the 1950s and 1960s, the change from the traditional *ie* system to a modern individual way of thinking, emancipation of women, etc. They are people whose values have gone through a complete revolution — experiences that the people of today's peaceful Japan will never face.

Among Japanese aged 65 or over 58 per cent are women. In 1980 60.1 per cent of women over 65 were widows. The figure for women aged over 75 is 78.7 per cent. The burden of a long life is especially hard for women. They are traditionally on the caring side, and after looking after their in-laws must take care of their husbands, later surviving them by 5-6 years.

With the growing ratio of the very old people, the number of bedridden old people is on the rise. In 1986 the number of bedridden Japanese elderly was around 600,000. In the year 2000 it is estimated to top one million. 250,000 bedridden elderly are hospitalized long term; 120,000 are being looked after in an old people's institution; 230,000 are being taken care of at home.

Taken care by whom? In nearly 40 cases out of 100, the person who looks after the well-being of the bedridden elderly is the daughter-in-law. The spouse of the patient is the one who takes care in 28 cases. In about 18 cases out of 100 the child of the ailing person is in charge. These are all figures stemming from a survey by the Ministry of Health and Welfare conducted in 1989.

Another group of the elderly is rapidly growing together with the aging of the society; the senile. In 1986 there were about 600,000 demented old people being taken care of at home. This number is also estimated to grow greatly toward the end of the century.

Recent trends in welfare for the aged

Jinsei hachijûnen — human life of 80 years — is the slogan in today's Japan. Most of all, the Japanese themselves are surprised and puzzled by the enormous speed in which their life span has grown. After the Second World War the average life span of the Japanese was around 50 years, now 40 years later, around 80. The nation of Japan is greying in a speed with no equal anywhere else in the world.

The ratio of the aged in Japan at the moment is around 12 per cent of the population — making Japan still a 'young' country compared with for instance Sweden's 17.6 per cent and England's 15.3 per cent. But the speed from now on is a quick one, in the year 2000 the percentage will be 16.3 per cent and in 2020 as high as 24 per cent. This means that a quarter of the population will be aged, 65 or older.

How to cope with this new kind of society is a question that the Japanese now have to ask themselves. The state has already started a few steps. The ten years from 1990 to 2000 are called 'The Ten Years to Promote Welfare and Health of the Aged'. Meanwhile, the Health and Medical Services Law for the Aged will be revised in the near future. The focus from now on will be on the many bedridden elderly who are taken care of by their families. In other words, how to ease the burden of the family.

No doubt, pensions have a large impact on the economic life of the elderly. Japan's pensions are on a par with those of Britain and the countries of Northern Europe, but for many elderly widows or divorcees who never drew a salary or had any other independent source of income, the pension level is low and in some cases these women have not been entitled to a pension at all. The amendment of the Pension Law of 1985 established the right of married women (including widowed and divorced women) to receive their own pensions.

Welfare of the aged in Japan

After the Second World War until 1963, the year of the establishment of the Law for the Welfare of the Aged, the substance of welfare for the aged was to fight against poverty, to help those with a lesser income (the Daily Security Law) and to give special help to the handicapped (the Invalid Law). From the 1960s until the early 1980s, while the nation's economy was rapidly developing, various services for the aged were introduced. Since 1966 September the

15th of each year is crowned 'A Day of Respect for the Aged'. Thus the new interest for the elderly was shown.

The Law for the Welfare of the Aged of 1963 came in due time under the very changed social circumstances of families and the elderly. The law contained the idea of duty of the local authorities to develop welfare of the aged, their health checks, support families, help the elderly to get into institutions and the like.

The year 1983 saw the implementation of the Health and Medical Services Law for the Aged. This law included medical checks for the elderly and some alterations to the previous law according to changed social and financial conditions. As the economy expanded, more and more taxes were channelled to the welfare of the aged. But in 1973 the oil crisis brought a temporary freezing of many a good plan.

The sudden economic downfall and rise in costs caused both the state and local governments an economic risk, delaying for instance the construction of new homes for the aged. Thus started a widespread discussion on how to continue working towards an aged society with lesser economic means.

Welfare — and how it is actually done

Welfare of the aged can be divided into two big categories: 1) care at home and 2) care at an institution. The first alternative has been traditionally predominant in Japan, the family taking care of the old person receiving practically no support at all from outside.

Even the elderly of tomorrow are still going to live with their offspring to a great extent, the care of the whole family has become a new target of welfare concerning the aged. With the pronunciation of The Ten Years to Promote Welfare and Health of the Aged, the state declared its Golden Plan for the next ten years to cope with the ever growing number of bedridden old people who are taken care of by their families.

The Golden Plan includes the 'Three Important Pillars' that enable the care of the elderly at home. These pillars are 1) home help service, 2) short stay service, and 3) day care service.

Home help service, which comprises the important work of home helpers and home makers, is still in its infancy in Japan. In a country with a population of 123 million there are only 31,405 home helpers (1989). The target of the Golden Plan is to increase this number to 100,000 by the end of the century.

As for the short stay service, the plan is to increase the number of beds from the present 4,274 (1989) to 50,000 till the year 2000. As far as the day care service is concerned, the government is planning to increase the number of day care centres from the present 1,080 (1989) to 10,000 by the end of this century. Also counselling services for families with aged persons will be a major target of increase.

Institutional care

While some Japanese have come to accept the idea of outside care for the aged, many still hesitate receiving such help. For many people, the word *rôjin hômu* (*rôjin*, aged, *hômu*, from the English word 'home') still has a negative sound reminding them of a poor house, *yôrôin*. One result from this is that many old people are sheltered in hospitals instead of nursing homes, because social mores endorse expert health care for the ailing, but reject nursing homes as a substitute for filial duty. This leads to the fact that about one third of the 250,000 patients aged 65, or over, have been hospitalized for over a year.

The Japanese homes for the aged are becoming the centres for welfare of the aged in their communities, as will be noticed later in the case of Shisei Home. Earlier they were shelters for the poor, now they are more and more becoming places for all the elderly citizens having a handicap of some sort, whether the people admit it or not. As Rojinfukushiron points, the present rôjin hômu must be looked from this point of view.

Live-in institutional welfare facilities for the elderly are classified into three types.

Yôgo hômu or homes for the aged with a low income are for those over 65 who have difficulties in receiving necessary care at home because of their physical or mental condition or because of the living environment. In 1988 there were about 70,000 elderly living in 944 yôgo homes in the whole country. Over two thirds (68 per cent) of them were public homes and the rest run by private persons or organizations.

The so-called *tokubetsu yôgo rôjin* home, special care home (*tokuyô hômu*) for the aged, is for those who due to a major physical or

179

mental disorder require constant supervision, which they cannot receive at home. In 1988 the capacity in the 1619 homes was about 120,000 people who were over 65 years of age. 80 per cent of tokuyoo homes are run by authority-assisted private organizations. The *keihi rôjin hômu*, low pay homes for the aged (or homes with moderate fees) are for those aged 60, or over, who receive less than a fixed level of income and who find it difficult to live at home because of family or housing circumstances.

In 1988 there were 280 keihi homes in Japan. 242 of them were the so-called keihi A type homes whose 14,712 residents pay only for the actual living costs, while management fees for instance are paid by authorities. In the 38 keihi B type homes all the costs are paid by residents themselves. In keihi B homes unlike keihi A homes no meals are served. Therefore in this case the term 'residential flat' would be a more suitable one.

In 1985 600,000 people of the Japanese elderly population needed regular nursing care. 250,000 of them were hospitalized long-term, 120,000 were looked after in special care homes (*tokuyô* homes) and the rest at their homes.

Many elderly are hospitalized not because of an illness but because they cannot receive proper care at home. In response to this situation health service facilities for the aged that are halfway between hospitals and welfare institutions have been established since 1986. These 'intermediate health care facilities', *rôjin hoken shisetsu*, have fewer doctors than hospitals have but more than special care homes. They are for patients who, before returning to their homes, need rehabilitation and adaptation together with care.

Entrance to a home for the aged depends on the nature of the home. The yôgo and tokuyô homes are entered by application to the local authorities, mainly the Welfare Board of town.

There are no economic limitations for entering a tokuyô home, the only criterion is being dependent both mentally and physically. A portion of the total cost of the care of the aged person is required to be paid by the person in question and his family according to their economic situation. The criteria are the same for the yôgo home: some people pay nothing, the others the total cost of care.

As for the keihi homes, the application is sent directly to the home. The fees that the residents pay depend on their income whose suitability is judged by the home. At the moment a typical keihi fee is around 20,000 yen per month. Keihi homes are for people who are not rich enough to enter silver business homes.

With the improvement of the pension system and thus the greater purchasing power of elderly people, various services outside the public ones have appeared. This kind of business whose target is the elderly population is called the 'Silver Business'.

The main silver business type are the so-called *yuuryô rôjin hômu*, high-pay live-in facilities whose number at the moment is around 150 (1988). A total of 14,428 people have chosen this fancy type of living in a home whose cost, at its best, may rise to tens of millions of yen at admission plus from one to two hundred thousand yen for various services per month.

The Silver Business is believed to stay there as an alternative for those who have means to buy these services, thus easing the burden in the public sector, but it will never be a total substitute for the welfare of the aged.

The same way as authority-assisted homes, also Silver Business homes have lately been targeted for inspection and checks for fear of possible malpractices. This means that the public sector has in a way approved the existence of this alternative in welfare for the aged.

Management of welfare for the aged

Article 25 of the Japanese Constitution states that the people of Japan are entitled to the right to spend a healthy and cultural life and the state has the obligation to work accordingly and promote the level of people's lives.

As it is said above, the state has the duty and obligation, but a great deal of the 'job' is done by the local authorities (the prefectural and municipal governments).

The Ministry of Health and Welfare has the last word and responsibility on the level of homes for the aged and other services. However, in the revision of The Law for the Welfare of the Aged (1990), both the responsibility and realisation of various services were put on the shoulders of the local governments.

Of the around 3000 authority-assisted homes for the aged, two thirds are run by private organizations. These non-profit organizations are seen to go on doing good work in the welfare field. The financial management of these institutions is carried half by the state and the other half by the prefectural and municipal government together. If a private organization wants to build a new home, half of the construction costs are carried by the state and local governments, one quarter by the prefecture and the rest by the organization itself. There may be differences between areas, and also frequently the actual cost paid by the organization is bigger than the numbers written on paper.

In turn to their support and assistance, the authorities have the right to make regular checks on the financial and other affairs of the homes. This is the miraculous 'marriage' between the authorities and private welfare organizations in Japan.

Institutional care — an example

Shisei Home in Tachikawa City, one-hour drive from downtown Tokyo, is a good example of the smooth cooperation, 'marriage' between the authorities and private welfare foundations.

Founded 40 years ago in 1951, Shisei Home shows all the energy and activity that is duly expected from a private non-profit institution in Japan. Starting residential services for 30 people six years after the end of the Second World War under the then Daily Security Law (later changed to the Law for the Welfare of the Aged) Shisei Home at present can boast of being a complete service centre for the aged in its community with residential services in three types of homes: yôgo home (60 beds), keihi A home (50 beds) and tokuyô home (140 beds). There is also a so-called care house (started in 1990), an apartment house with care services and 15 rooms, a day care home, short stay services, bathing and meal services, a day home for the senile as well as a clinic with 19 beds. Shisei Home is a complex where the elderly people's all needs are taken care of. They even need not go to hospital to die — for most of them, the Shisei clinic is the place where they die.

A total of 200 competent, mostly young staff mind the needs of the aged. One quarter of the staff has already taken (passed) the qualification for workers of social institutions stipulated by the 1988 Certified Social Worker and Certified Care Worker Law. This law is believed to unify more and more the level of the welfare for the aged as well as to improve the image of welfare work and the morale of workers.

Shisei Home is in cooperation and mutual assisting relationship with Tachikawa City, where it is situated, and four other neighbourly towns, giving services and, in turn, being funded by them.

The average age of the residents is 81.2 years, depending slightly on the type of home; the tokuyô home has the oldest residents, the average being 82.3 years (1991).

The ratio of women to men in yôgo home is 45 to 15, in keihi home 39 to 21 and in tokuyô home 110 to 30.

In addition to the staff of 200, including 2 doctors, rehabilitation specialists, nutritionists, who keep the menu for the aged healthy, around 4500 volunteers per year, mainly middle-aged women, come to Shisei Home to lend a hand. The number of elderly volunteers from the neighbouring community is also increasing.

They chose like Mr. O.

a.

Mrs. T. was born in 1904 as a daughter of a bushi warrior in Kanda, downtown Tokyo. She was one of the family's four children and was compelled to leave school after three years of studies. After school she became an au pair in a family. At the age of 18 Mrs. T. got married and gave birth to five children, of whom four survived. When she was 31, her husband died in a traffic accident. The children were 9, 7, 4 and 1 at the time. In order to support her children she tried different kinds of jobs in the selling business.

The eldest son died in the Second World War, which caused a tremendous pain to her. Two of her daughters are still alive. Mrs. T. had never been in very good terms with her second daughter, therefore she hoped she could live with her third daughter. But as this daughter left home to get married, Mrs. T. gave up the idea of living together with her and lived alone until the age of 67.

She then sold the tiny shop she owned, gave the money to her third daughter and moved into her place. In return for having a place to live, she helped the family economy by giving her pension as well as the allowance of her war-dead son to her daughter.

When Mrs. T. was 80 the daughter's health deteriorated and she went by herself to the local welfare office to get advice. She asked to be admitted to a home for the aged. On hearing this the daughter became furious. However, five months later, Mrs. T. found herself in Shisei yôgo home.

Mrs. T.'s pension totals 330,000 yen a year. Besides, she receives a total of 1.525,940 yen a year as pension for her son who died in the war. Mrs. T.'s monthly payment for residence at Shisei Home which is determined by her income is 104,700 yen.

Nevertheless, the relations with the daughter's family are good. The death of her son is still on her mind and she goes yearly to Yasukuni Shrine (the resting place for the dead in the war) to pray for his soul.

Although seemingly in poor physical condition, Mrs. T. is mentally active for her age. She enjoys various activities in the home, as if showing the people that she is independent and free to do whatever she wants to. Having had only three years of education Mrs. T., although slightly backward in knowledge, has a tremendous wish to learn new things. She, among other things, surprised her fellow residents by joining the English conversation class of yôgo home. Feeling that she is independent and not a burden to anyone, she keeps on saying to people around her, 'This is the best place where I have ever been'.

b.

Mrs. M. was born in Pusan, Korea, in 1908, the eldest of three children of a Japanese tax accountant. When she was three years old, her father was transferred to Dailien, Manchuria, where she attended a girls' school and eventually became a typist-stenographer. She then worked for the South Manchuria Railways and was a teacher at a typists' school. At 28, she married a Japanese vice-chairman of a trade company, gave birth to a son and a daughter, and led a prosperous life.

After the war the family moved to Tokyo where the husband got work in a ball pen factory. On their way back to Japan in a terrible chaos the son died, and as a result of a shock Mrs. M. lost her hearing. Back in Tokyo, at the age of 42, she gave birth to another baby boy. It was a difficult delivery. Mrs. M. started working again, this time as a conference stenographer, but because of bad hearing had to quit this job soon. After that she tried various jobs, such as gathering advertisements.

After retirement in 1971 her husband started a printing press of his own. They worked together in this enterprise until his death three years later.

After the husband's death Mrs. M. continued the family business with her son-in-law. She lived in a council house apartment alone, but when the son got married in 1979, she moved to his house. Due to bad relations with her daughter-in-law three years later she rented an apartment near her daughter's house.

When Mrs. M. noticed that her life alone was getting more and more difficult, she went to Shisei Home to discuss the possibility of moving into the keihi A home. But because of her bad hearing and walking problems, she was instead advised to try entrance into the yôgo home. Finally she decided on continuing to live in her apartment and attend the day care home for the aged where she received rehabilitation among other activities.

Life went on like this for a year and a half, after which she was admitted to the yôgo home. Even at the yôgo home she fell to the category of the weakest people and eventually sent an application to be admitted to the tokuyoo home. Being a proud person and unwilling to show weakness Mrs. M. decided to try to get her legs treated and entered a hospital for an operation of legs. During the operation, however, she suffered a heart attack and had to stay in hospital for several months. Finally, she entered the tokuyoo home and is still an active member of several hobby groups. Her bad hearing, however, make human relations difficult for her.

Mrs. M. was unable to get along with the family members under the same roof. But she was never rejected by the family, they were always by her side whatever she decided to do. Mrs. M. takes pride in herself, what she is and what she has done. She wants to decide on her own way of life till the very end. She wants to know 100 percent where she stands. She may be the model for tomorrow's Japanese elderly who want to decide on their money, living place and way of life.

c.

The third example is the case of an aged man, Mr. K., who was born in 1907. He is a big man with a big smile. He lives under the same roof with his wife and the family of his son. The married grandson also lives in the same house with his wife. Mr. K is daily taken care of by his 67-year-old wife.

Mr. K. had a brain haemorrhage 12 years ago. What is left of that illness today is a paralysed right side, hearing difficulties and a speech defect. After the stroke Mr. K. stayed in hospital for a month. Since then he has been looked after at home, at the same time receiving rehabilitation and other services at the local Shisei Day Care Home for the Aged. Soon after the stroke he attended only bathing services, gradually, however, transferred to day care home and short-stay programmes. Now he is quite capable of doing simple daily jobs by himself. Now he can even take a bath at home.

Mr. K. has difficulties in communicating with people, but he, nevertheless, eagerly attends the activities of the day care home with other elderly people. His favourite is the pottery class. He still has regular physical therapy sessions, as well as occupational and speech therapy.

Seeing Mr. K. handle clay with his left hand in the pottery class is an amazing scene, a real show of courage and hidden human energy.

This gentleman has been able to live at home with his loved ones in spite of his handicap for over ten years, thanks to the warm family relations, his zeal for independence, his optimism, the many possibilities that the short-stay and day care home services give a family, and rehabilitation that strengthens the independence of man.

Why institutional care is needed besides home care

Even though short-stay and related services which were mentioned in Mr. K.'s case, proved that, if an aged person receives proper care, treatment and help from outside, the ideal place for him is his own home, to live there alone or with relatives, as long as possible, there are still many obstacles to this kind of state of affairs in Japan.

In the first place, the Japanese family situation has changed. Women, on whose shoulders the care and welfare of the sick and elderly has traditionally been, have started to go out to work. In 1988 48.9 per cent of all women were engaged in work outside home.

Secondly, Japanese housing conditions pose many obstacles. Steps and uneven floors, hallways where wheelchairs cannot be used, and the small size of the Japanese homes, especially in metropolitan areas, combine to deprive convalescents of opportunities to movement at home and make it difficult for them to regain independence. The poor state of Japanese housing leads to results in an increase of medically unnecessary hospitalization and institutionalized care.

According to a survey conducted in Hyogo Prefecture in 1988 among inhabitants of yôgo homes, 34 per cent entered the place because of family circumstances, 19 per cent because of physical disabilities, 16 per cent due to their housing situation, and 16 per cent for economic reasons. Among those who entered special care homes 60 per cent entered the place because of physical disabilities and 24 per cent because of family circumstances. As for those living in keihi homes, 43 per cent entered the home because of family circumstances, and 36 per cent because of their housing situation. Although the percentage of people living in homes for the elderly for housing reasons is not very high, lack of adequate housing may have been a subsidiary factor for those who cited economic or family circumstances.

In this survey, the residents were also asked whether they had a home where they could return. 78 per cent of the residents of yôgo homes, 59 per cent of those in special care homes and 45 per cent of those in keihi homes said they did not have one. While there are differences among the institutions, the greatest number of those who said they had no home to return to had no family members with whom to live before entering these facilities. Approximately 20 per cent from each cited physical disability, housing conditions, and strained family relationships.

Among those respondents who cited housing conditions as the first or second reason for entering an institution, the most often mentioned reasons for finding it difficult to live at home were its small size and too many people living in it; steps and uneven floors; inadequate toilet, kitchen or bathing facilities and lack of sunlight. Naturally these factors most severely affected residents of special care homes who, due to physical or mental disabilities, require constant supervision. Noteworthy is the fact that 50 per cent of those in yôgo homes who entered the place because of housing circumstances mentioned the smallness of their former residences. In other words, inadequate living space is the most important reason for entering such facilities when a person is without serious physical or mental disabilities.

Just as important as improving facilities, homes and service centres for the elderly, however, is the creation of housing conditions that preclude the need for institutionalized care. If adequate housing conditions are not realized, satisfactory home care will never become possible in Japan, and the effectiveness of pensions, medical treatment, and other social security programmes and services will be lost.

Finally

As was mentioned above, residential services for the aged have their roots deep in Japan, but recently, different needs from residential homes have arisen. Therefore, the nature of an institution has changed. So the homes have developed each retaining its own characteristics.

Now that people are living longer and longer and the rate of the very old is rapidly increasing, at the same time increasing the number of the sick and bedridden people, the term 'care' has become a topic for discussion. The home for the aged has become the centre of residential care and open care for those living at home. Especially as the need for old people's apartments and residential flats has increased, care service and meal service needs have emerged from the home for the aged.

The Central Social Welfare Advisory Committee submitted a paper in 1989 concerning the situation of homes for the aged. It recommended the introduction of a type of facility to be called the 'care house' (like the one at Shisei Home) that emphasizes both residential and welfare qualities. The coordination of welfare and residential policies is considered to become even more important from now on.

What is important now in Japan, besides increasing facilities, various social services, improving housing conditions, etc., is the mutual understanding and cooperation between authorities and the people concerning the needs of an aged Japan of the 21st century. The *Fukushi Vision*, a vision of a state where the elderly can lead a happy and care-free life, as was declared the aim of the Government in 1988, is still behind the corner. Whether it will be reached by the year 2000, depends now on the Japanese themselves and their understanding of society and welfare.

Anyway, what the Japanese are now looking for is the fruit of their postwar prosperity. It should have an impact on their daily lives, and not least on their old age. Or should the creators of this great Japanese prosperity, the elderly of today and tomorrow, be forgotten?

References

Hashimoto, Masaaki (1990), *Rôjin to fukushi*, (Shakai-fukushi no taisho to bunya I), Tôkyô.

Hashimoto, Masaaki (1990), 'Kôrei-shakai ni sonaeru yutakana chôju-sha. Kai eno Love Call', *Shisei Home Pamphlet* No. 1.

Hayakawa, Kazuo (1990), 'Housing for the Elderly', *Gerontology: New Horizon*, vol. 1.

'Kyojû-jôken to shippei no kankei' (1988), Sôgô Shakai Hoshô, October.

Naoi, Michiko & Hashimoto, Masaaki (eds.) (1990), *Rojin-fukushiron*, Discussions on Old People's Welfare, Shakai-fukushi-senmonshoku Library, Seishin Shobô, Tokyo.

Rôjin-hoken-iryô to Fukushi (1991), Seido no gaiyô to dôkô, Ministry of Health and Welfare Publication.

Time Magazine (1989), August 28th, 1989.

White Paper on Health and Welfare (1988), Ministry of Health and Welfare; and several newspaper articles.

10 Minsei-iin community volunteers – an important network in the field of welfare in Japan

Raija Hashimoto

Needless to say, one of the most extraordinary systems in the field of welfare in Japan is the Minsei-iin Community Volunteer network. With a history going back to the beginning of this century, or even further, the network currently boasts nearly 200,000 members all over the country. The Minsei-iin volunteers are said to be an irreplaceable link between the authorities and residents, people in need. It is the most brilliant example of neighbourly love and responsibility turned into help in this eastern nation.

Mrs. F. H. (71) has been a Minsei-iin volunteer since 1974. A dietician by education, she worked in a home for the aged, first as a dietician and social worker, later as the director, for 40 years until her retirement at the age of 70.

How do you become a Minsei-iin volunteer?

FH: We, the Minsei-iin community volunteers (*minsei* means 'public welfare', thus we can be said to be 'public welfare commissioners'), are officially appointed by the Minister of Health and Welfare, but we are actually chosen and invited to this task by the Board to Choose Minsei-iin of each town or ward. The board looks for suitable persons. The word 'suitable' in this context means someone who is of a responsible type, who is independent economically, who has the will to help and promote community life in a positive way, and who is of proper age (proper age meaning under 65 years when appointed for the first time and under 73 when reappointed). Both men and women are recruited. The man-woman ratio in

190

my home town, T. City, is 58:65. This is not a job for women only, as often is the case when we talk about voluntary work. But it is a fact that it is very hard for a man who works full time to become a volunteer because of the long office hours. Therefore most Minsei-iin volunteers, both men and women, are self-employed, run some kind of business themselves and can decide about their use of time freely.

According to the Minsei-iin Handbook, the Minsei-iin are voluntary workers, as stated in the Minsei-iin Law promulgated in 1948. The term of service is 3 years, but it can be extended a number of times. Most Minsei-iin are said to be in service for 10 years on average, as experience really counts in this work.

According to the 1986 statistics, 59.8 per cent of Minsei-iin were men and 40.2 per cent women. The biggest age group was from 51 to 60 years (42.5 per cent). People with ages ranging from 61 to 70 accounted for 38.6 per cent of the total. As for occupation, 35.9 per cent were unemployed (retired, etc.), 27.6 per cent were engaged in agriculture and 17.9 per cent were self-employed. The Minsei-iin make a pledge to improve community life and the living conditions of residents in their area. They devote themselves to those in need of help and advice. Consequently, the Minsei-iin should be self-motivated to serve others and be service-minded without expecting a reward. They should also work for the betterment of the entire community, together with co-residents, conveying the people's feelings to the authorities and serving as mediators between the authorities and social institutions, and residents.

FH: Our tasks are many. We offer various forms of assistance to residents in cooperation with public welfare officials. In accordance with the Child Welfare Law, we also serve as volunteers working in the field of children's affairs.

First, we make surveys of the living conditions of residents and their welfare problems. I think we Minsei-iin know better the circumstances of, say, the elderly and children in our respective areas than any other people or any social agency. Secondly, we act as liaison between residents and relevant agencies. Another important task is making proposals to the authorities on behalf of the residents for improving their living conditions.

We try to take a close look at our specific areas. We try to see the whole situation concerning people's living conditions, be they young or old, handicapped or lonely. If we find some fault, we'll tackle it.

As of 1983, there are 174,065 Minsei-iin volunteers in the whole of Japan. In Tokyo and other metropolitan areas, there is one Minsei-iin for every 270 families. In a city with a population of over 100,000, the ratio is one for every 200 families, and in smaller towns and villages, one for every 120 families.

FH: In some regions, the number of Minsei-iin is in accordance with the recommendation, but in my area, for example, with 700 families, there are only two of us, a gentleman and I.

Do you get any pay for your work?

FH: We are volunteers and do not expect any pay for the work we do, but nowadays we receive a nominal 'travel fee' which is about 100,000 yen per year. This amounts to about one third of the monthly salary of an office clerk. Also, this is a small compensation for having to make a lot of telephone calls. I myself am against all payments — we are volunteers!

Your work schedule as a Minsei-iin?

FH: I am involved in Minsei-iin activities for about 10 days a month. It is not especially much, it is about the average. People come to see me and I also visit them. We make a monthly report to the local Minsei-iin council of our activities. By the way, it is possible to be dismissed from this position, if your work is not satisfactory!

According to the Minsei-iin Handbook (1989), the total number of active days per month for the Minsei-iin was 9.2 days per person in 1988. They made 18.8 visits per month on average.

The biggest task, by far, is consultation and guidance which amounts to 6.0 times a month per Minsei-iin. Surveys average 2.4 times, contacts to related institutions 3.0, attendance to events 4.3, friendly visits 3.6 and legal matters (such as certifying eligibility for living allowances) 0.3 (as of 1988).

192

Of the consultation cases, 32.2 per cent are related to matters of health. Family problems stand at 7.0 per cent, housing at 5.0 per cent, living environment at 7.1 per cent, family budget at 8.0 per cent, matters concerning work at 3.8 per cent, delinquent protection at 3.0 per cent, and other matters at 30.8 per cent (1988).

In the Tokyo area (1988), 18 per cent of consultation cases deal with old age, 14 per cent with children's affairs and single parent families, 5 per cent with handicapped and their problems and 9 per cent with other matters. This is a welfare perspective of the statistics.

About Minsei-iin history? How far are its roots?

FH: Actually the Minsei-iin organization has been there, I mean with the name of Minsei-iin, since 1946, when the Minsei-iin Community Volunteer Ordinance was promulgated. The Minsei-iin Community Volunteer Law is from the year 1948. But the system of neighbourhood help has been there much, much longer. The idea can be traced as far back as the Heian period about 800 years ago, when we had the so called *hiden-in* system which ordered the landlord to look after his subjects like a father looks after his children. In the Edo period, people gave seven per cent of their crops to a special relief fund which was used to help people in distress, the poor, the old, the lonely, widows, orphans and the like. The first Minsei-iin-like organization was inaugurated in Okayama Prefecture, south of Osaka, in 1917. The so called *Homen-iin* (district volunteer) system saw daylight in Japan the following year, 1918. During the next 10 years this system spread all over the country, having 15,000 volunteers by 1928. After the war, the District Volunteer System was then restarted as the Minsei-iin Community Volunteer System, as I mentioned above.

Ever since the promulgation of the Daily Life Security Law (1946), the Minsei-iin volunteers have been a collaborative resource of the municipal level public welfare administration in providing care services.

Specifically, what do you do as a Minsei-iin in your area?

FH: As I said earlier, we keep an eye on our area. We know what the situation is. On behalf of the local government, we take an account of the elderly. We see how many of them live with their families, how many live alone. We make surveys of their life conditions and inform the city of our findings. In the autumn, before the September 15th Respect for the Aged Day, we visit all the elderly in the area and personally bring them the yearly money gift from the local government (5000 yen for those over 70 years of age and 10,000 yen for those over 75). This may sound very irrational as the money could be sent via mail, but in this way, we keep in touch with the people. Some towns have already changed to the mail service, not relying on the Minsei-iin in this respect. We also deliver the so called Silver Pass tickets (free bus tickets) to over 70-year-old people, as well as bath house tickets issued by the local government. Sometimes these visits are very hard — climbing to the third or fourth floor on foot and meeting no one at home, thus having to go again on the following day! And most of us Minsei-iin are not young any more.

We also deliver information about services to the people. We are contact persons. We find a volunteer to lend a hand or we alert home helps.

What about children? You are said to have an important role in welfare for the children, too.

FH: Yes, we tackle many problems of the younger generation, too. Let's mention juvenile delinquency, and problems of single-parent and divorce families; these problems are on the rise in Japan. Some of us are appointed exclusively to deal with the problems of the young. The Minsei-iin Council includes a special Committee for Matters of the Young. School absenteeism and school fear have lately become much discussed topics.

What kind of network do you have inside the Minsei-iin system?

FH: Well, we have two ways of acting. First of all, we may act on our own, as individuals; and secondly, we may act as a group. There is a Minsei-iin Volunteer Council in each town and village, including a Counselling Centre where people can come to meet us. In the Council there is a person and his or her deputy who deal with general affairs. Then one of us takes on the position of the cashier. And one of us is elected as the representative of our organization in town. This person is usually appointed by the town. There is a National Council, as well.

We, the Minsei-iin, deal with all kinds of affairs of the community, but one thing is forbidden: we cannot take part in politics. We must be apolitical persons with no affiliations.

What would you say are the problems in your work as a Minsei-iin?

FH: The problems are often related to how people understand community life and our work. Once I visited an old lady who only wanted somebody to clean her garden. I contacted the Retired People's Gardener Service but when a gardener came to her house, she said she has no money to pay for the job, which was a mere 6,000 yen for a day. There was nothing else for me to do but to get a couple of other Minsei-iin to help and start cleaning the garden! And that is not our work! Our work is to provide information and arrange for somebody else to come and help. For some work the people pay, for work done by volunteers they don't.

We also meet a lot of misunderstanding and stupid pride from the families of the elderly, handicapped and so on. Still today, the last thing many people want is help from society. 'We can manage,' is many times the answer from an unmarried son of a bed-ridden old person. Sad, isn't it?

Also, much depends on ourselves, on our own character. We have to be wise. We must have life experience. Therefore it is good not to be too young. Imagine a young male Minsei-iin taking care of a family of a mother and child! What problems might occur! The more frictionless you want the relationship between the people and authorities to be, the wiser and the more experienced you yourself will have to be.

Good points about being a Minsei-iin?

FH: For me it has been a most rewarding experience. Earlier, working only inside the home for the aged, I knew nothing but the home for the aged. Through this work I have learnt a lot about the surrounding community and the many-stringed network that it has. I have learnt to know the town where I live and work. I planned to give up my Minsei-iin status when I retired, but I am still here!

References

The Minsei-iin Handbook (*Minsei-iin, Jidô-iin no tebiki*) (1989), Tokyo Metropolitan Government.
Minsei-iin (1986), The Japanese National Council of Minsei-iin Community. Child Welfare Volunteers.

Notes on contributors

Ingrid Getreuer-Kargl

Dr Getreuer-Kargl graduated from the University of Vienna with a doctoral dissertation on 'Hospitalization of the Mentally Ill in Japan' and afterwards worked on a project 'Consequences of and Reactions to the Ageing of Society in Japan'. She is at present assistant and lecturer at the Institute of Japanology of the University of Vienna, with main research interests in gender studies.
Address: Institute for Japanese Studies
          University of Vienna
          Universitätsstraße 7
          A-1010 Vienna, Austria

Raija Hashimoto

Ms Hashimoto lives in Tokyo where she works as a translator and a voluntary worker at Shisei Home whose director her husband is. Raija Hashimoto has graduated from the University of Jyväskylä in Finland, and has studied at the International Christian University of Tokyo.
Address: 6-8-2 Nishiko-cho
          Tachikawa-shi
          Tokyo 190, Japan

Liisa Knuuti

Ms Knuuti is a researcher and social scientist, with a degree (MSc) in social psychology. Her PhD studies at the University of Helsinki focus on 'Postmodernism and City Culture in Finland'. Publications on the same theme: an article in the Publications of the University of Helsinki 'Postmodernism and Urban Lifestyle' and a paper in AESOP (Association of European Schools of Planning-Congress) entitled 'Urban Lifestyles and City Planning in Finland'. Ms Knuuti works as a planner of postgraduate education in the Centre for Urban and Regional Studies at the Helsinki University of Technology. She is a contact person in Finland with NORDPLAN.

Address: Centre for Urban and Regional Studies
Helsinki University of Technology
Otakaari 1
02150 Espoo, Finland

Briitta Koskiaho

Professor of Social Policy at the University of Tampere. Her current interests include problems of the ageing society and urban questions. Together with Japanese colleagues she has done research on the ageing society in Finland and in Japan. Recent publications on Japan include articles on the industrialization and restructuring of Japan and two books written in Finnish on the Japanese society ('Englannin perässäkulkijatko?' Gaudeamus-Kirja, Helsinki 1995, and 'Japani, yhteiskunnan murros'. Painatuskeskus Oy, Helsinki 1995).

Address: Department of Social Policy and Social Work
University of Tampere
P.O. Box 607
33101 Tampere, Finland

Machiko Osawa

Machiko Osawa, Professor of Economics, Asia University in Tokyo. She was formerly a researcher at the Japan Institute of Labor. Earned her PhD at Southern Illinois University and completed a post-doctorate at the University of Chicago. Her book 'Economic Change and Working Women in Japan and the U.S.' (in Japanese) received the 1994 Kagami Award for the Best Book in Economics.

Address: Asia University
          Tokyo, Japan

Sachiko Matsumura

Dr Matsumura, Professor of Social Planning, Gunma University, lives in Tokyo. She is involved in questions of social policy in many practical ways, too.

Address: Gunma University
          Gunma, Japan

Maija-Liisa Pättiniemi

Ms Pättiniemi works as a research fellow in the Department of Social Policy at the University of Tampere. She has studied the changing of female textile workers' life and housing careers and is preparing her doctoral dissertation on the elderly people's housing and services. Published on this theme 'Kotini vai linnani?' (1995) in the series of the Ministry of the Environment in Finnish, and articles in English.

Address: Department of Social Policy and Social Work
          University of Tampere
          P.O. Box 607
          33101 Tampere, Finland

Mirja Tolkki-Nikkonen

Dr Tolkki-Nikkonen, Associate Professor of Social Psychology at the University of Tampere. Her current research interests are in family rhetorics, questions of social identity and new methodological orientations. With her Nordic colleagues she has studied intact married couples. Recent publications include social identity and articles and books on Finnish families and married couples.

Address: Department of Sociology and Social Psychology
          University of Tampere
          P.O. Box 607
          33101 Tampere, Finland